# Mental Health Act 1983

**CHAPTER 20**

Explanatory Notes are available separately

**GRAN*GIS* UK Publishing**

Adapted and published by GRANGIS (Grand Register Library).
Online: www.grangis.com
E-mail: contact@grangis.com


In this version:
ISBN: 979-8-88559-027-3

Note: This is the original version (as it was originally enacted). Title, sub-title and the generated date is as marked on the pages.

# Mental Health Act 1983

## CHAPTER 20

## MENTAL HEALTH ACT 1983

### PART I

APPLICATION OF ACT



### PART II

COMPULSORY ADMISSION TO HOSPITAL AND GUARDIANSHIP

*Procedure for hospital admission*



*Guardianship*



*General provisions as to applications and recommendations*

## PART X

MISCELLANEOUS AND SUPPLEMENTARY

*Miscellaneous provisions*



*Supplemental*



---

SCHEDULES

# Mental Health Act 1983

## 1983 CHAPTER 20

An Act to consolidate the law relating to mentally disordered persons. [9th May 1983]

BE IT ENACTED by the Queen's most Excellent Majesty, by and with the advice and consent of the Lords Spiritual and Temporal, and Commons, in this present Parliament assembled, and by the authority of the same, as follows:—

## PART I

### APPLICATION OF ACT

**1 Application of Act: " mental disorder "**

(1) The provisions of this Act shall have effect with respect to the reception, care and treatment of mentally disordered patients, the management of their property and other related matters.

(2) In this Act—

"mental disorder" means mental illness, arrested or incomplete development of mind, psychopathic disorder and any other disorder or disability of mind and " mentally disordered" shall be construed accordingly;

" severe mental impairment" means a state of arrested or incomplete development of mind which includes severe impairment of intelligence and social functioning and is associated with abnormally aggressive or seriously irresponsible conduct on the part of the person concerned and "severely mentally impaired" shall be construed accordingly;

" mental impairment" means a state of arrested or incomplete development of mind (not amounting to severe mental impairment) which includes significant impairment of intelligence and social functioning and is associated with abnormally aggressive or seriously irresponsible conduct on the part of the person concerned and "mentally impaired" shall be construed accordingly;

"psychopathic disorder" means a persistent disorder or disability of mind (whether or not including significant impairment of intelligence) which results in abnormally aggressive or seriously irresponsible conduct on the part of the person concerned;

and other expressions shall have the meanings assigned to them in section 145 below.

(3) Nothing in subsection (2) above shall be construed as implying that a person may be dealt with under this Act as suffering from mental disorder, or from any form of mental disorder described in this section, by reason only of promiscuity or other immoral conduct, sexual deviancy or dependence on alcohol or drugs.

## PART II

### Compulsory Admission to Hospital and Guardianship

*Procedure for hospital admission*

### 2 Admission for assessment

(1) A patient may be admitted to a hospital and detained there for the period allowed by subsection (4) below in pursuance of an application (in this Act referred to as "an application for admission for assessment") made in accordance with subsections (2) and (3) below.

(2) An application for admission for assessment may be made in respect of a patient on the grounds that—

(a) he is suffering from mental disorder of a nature or degree which warrants the detention of the patient in a hospital for assessment (or for assessment followed by medical treatment) for at least a limited period ; and

(b) he ought to be so detained in the interests of his own health or safety or with a view to the protection of other persons.

(3) An application for admission for assessment shall be founded on the written recommendations in the prescribed form of two registered medical practitioners, including in each case a statement that in the opinion of the practitioner the conditions set out in subsection (2) above are complied with.

(4) Subject to the provisions of section 29(4) below, a patient admitted to hospital in pursuance of an application for admission for assessment may be detained for a period not exceeding 28 days beginning with the day on which he is admitted, but shall not be detained after the expiration of that period unless before it has expired he has become liable to be detained by virtue of a subsequent application, order or direction under the following provisions of this Act.

### 3 Admission for treatment

(1) A patient may be admitted to a hospital and detained there for the period allowed by the following provisions of this Act in pursuance of an application (in this Act referred to as "an application for admission for treatment") made in accordance with this section.

(2) An application for admission for treatment may be made in respect of a patient on the grounds that—

(a) he is suffering from mental illness, severe mental impairment, psychopathic disorder or mental impairment and his mental disorder is of a nature or degree which makes it appropriate for him to receive medical treatment in a hospital; and

(b) in the case of psychopathic disorder or mental impairment, such treatment is likely to alleviate or prevent a deterioration of his condition; and

(c) it is necessary for the health or safety of the patient or for the protection of other persons that he should receive such treatment and it cannot be provided unless he is detained under this section.

(3) An application for admission for treatment shall be founded on the written recommendations in the prescribed form! of two registered medical practitioners, including in each case a statement that in the opinion of the practitioner the conditions set out in subsection (2) above are complied with; and each such recommendation shall include—

(a) such particulars as may be prescribed of the grounds for that opinion so far as it relates to the conditions set out in paragraphs (a) and (b) of that subsection; and

(b) a statement of the reasons for that opinion so far as it relates to the conditions set out in paragraph (c) of that subsection, specifying whether other methods of dealing with the patient are available and, if so, why they are not appropriate.

## 4 Admission for assessment in cases of emergency

(1) In any case of urgent necessity, an application for admission for assessment may be made in respect of a patient in accordance with the following provisions of this section, and any application so made is in this Act referred to as " an emergency application ".

(2) An emergency application may be made either by an approved social worker or by the nearest relative of the patient; and every such application shall include a statement that it is of urgent necessity for the patient to be admitted and detained under section 2 above, and that compliance with the provisions of this Part of this Act relating to applications under that section would involve undesirable delay.

(3) An emergency application shall be sufficient in the first instance if founded on one of the medical recommendations required by section 2 above, given, if practicable, by a practitioner who has previous acquaintance with the patient and otherwise complying with the requirements of section 12 below so far as applicable to a single recommendation, and verifying the statement referred to in subsection (2) above.

(4) An emergency application shall cease to have effect on the expiration of a period of 72 hours from the time when the patient is admitted to the hospital unless—

(a) the second medical recommendation required by section 2 above is given and received by the managers within that period ; and

(b) that recommendation and the recommendation referred to in subsection (3) above together comply with all the requirements of section 12 below (other than the requirement as to the time of signature of the second recommendation).

(5) In relation to an emergency application, section 11 below shall have effect as if in subsection (5) of that section for the words " the period of 14 days ending with the date of the application " there were substituted the words " the previous 24 hours " .

## 5 Application in respect of patient already in hospital

(1) An application for the admission of a patient to a hospital may be made under this Part of this Act notwithstanding that the patient is already an in-patient in that hospital or, in the case of an application for admission for treatment that the patient is for the time being liable to be detained in the hospital in pursuance of an application for admission for assessment; and where an application is so made the patient shall be treated for the purposes of this Part of this Act as if he had been admitted to the hospital at the time when that application was received by the managers.

(2) If, in the case of a patient who is an in-patient in a hospital, it appears to the registered medical practitioner in charge of the treatment of the patient that an application ought to be made under this Part of this Act for the admission of the patient to hospital, he may furnish to the managers a report in writing to that effect; and in any such case the patient may be detained in the hospital for a period of 72 hours from the time when the report is so furnished.

(3) The registered medical practitioner in charge of the treatment of a patient in a hospital may nominate one (but not more than one) other registered medical practitioner on the staff of that hospital to act for him under subsection (2) above in his absence.

(4) If, in the case of a patient who is receiving treatment for mental disorder as an in-patient in a hospital, it appears to a nurse of the prescribed class—

(a) that the patient is suffering from mental disorder to such a degree that it is necessary for his health or safety or for the protection of others for him to be immediately restrained from leaving the hospital; and

(b) that it is not practicable to secure the immediate attendance of a practitioner for the purpose of furnishing a report under subsection (2) above,

the nurse may record that fact in writing; and in that event the patient may be detained in the hospital for a period of six hours from the time when that fact is so recorded or until the earlier arrival at the place where the patient is detained of a practitioner having power to furnish a report under that subsection.

(5) A record made under subsection (4) above shall be delivered by the nurse (or by a person authorised by the nurse in that behalf) to the managers of the hospital as soon as possible after it is made; and where a record is made under that subsection the period mentioned in subsection (2) above shall begin at the time when it is made.

(6) The reference in subsection (1) above to an in-patient does not include an in-patient who is liable to be detained in pursuance of an application under this Part of this Act and the references in subsections (2) and (4) above do not include an in-patient who is liable to be detained in a hospital under this Part of this Act.

(7) In subsection (4) above " prescribed" means prescribed by an order made by the Secretary of State.

## 6 Effect of application for admission

(1) An application for the admission of a patient to a hospital under this Part of this Act, duly completed in accordance with the provisions of this Part of this Act, shall be sufficient authority for the applicant, or any person authorised by the applicant, to take the patient and convey him to the hospital at any time within the following period, that is to say—

(a) in the case of an application other than an emergency application, the period of 14 days beginning with the date on which the patient was last examined by a registered medical practitioner before giving a medical recommendation for the purposes of the application;

(b) in the case of an emergency application, the period of 24 hours beginning at the time when the patient was examined by the practitioner giving the medical recommendation which is referred to in section 4(3) above, or at the time when the application is made, whichever is the earlier.

(2) Where a patient is admitted within the said period to the hospital specified in such an application as is mentioned in subsection (1) above, or, being within that hospital, is treated by virtue of section 5 above as if he had been so admitted, the application shall be sufficient authority for the managers to detain the patient in the hospital in accordance with the provisions of this Act.

(3) Any application for the admission of a patient under this Part of this Act which appears to be duly made and to be founded on the necessary medical recommendations may be acted upon without further proof of the signature or qualification of the person by whom the application or any such medical recommendation is made or given or of any matter of fact or opinion stated in it.

(4) Where a patient is admitted to a hospital in pursuance of an application for admission for treatment, any previous application under this Part of this Act by virtue of which he was liable to be detained in a hospital or subject to guardianship shall cease to have effect.

### *Guardianship*

## 7 Application for guardianship

(1) A patient who has attained the age of 16 years may be received into guardianship, for the period allowed by the following provisions of this Act, in pursuance of an application (in this Act referred to as " a guardianship application ") made in accordance with this section.

(2) A guardianship application may be made in respect of a patient on the grounds that—

(a) he is suffering from mental disorder, being mental illness, severe mental impairment, psychopathic disorder or mental impairment and his mental disorder is of a nature or degree which warrants his reception into guardianship under this section; and

(b) it is necessary in the interests of the welfare of the patient or for the protection of other persons that the patient should be so received.

(3) A guardianship application shall be founded on the written recommendations in the prescribed form of two registered medical practitioners, including in each case a statement that in the opinion of the practitioner the conditions set out in subsection (2) above are complied with; and each such recommendation shall include—

(a) such particulars as may be prescribed of the grounds for that opinion so far as it relates to the conditions set out in paragraph (a) of that subsection; and

(b) a statement of the reasons for that opinion so far as it relates to the conditions set out in paragraph (b) of that subsection.

(4) A guardianship application shall state the age of the patient or, if his exact age is not known to the applicant, shall state (if it be the fact) that the patient is believed to have attained the age of 16 years.

(5) The person named as guardian in a guardianship application may be either a local social services authority or any other person (including the applicant himself); but a guardianship application in which a person other than a local social services authority is named as guardian shall be of no effect unless it is accepted on behalf of that person by the local social services authority for the area in which he resides, and shall be accompanied by a statement in writing by that person that he is willing to act as guardian.

### 8 Effect of guardianship application, etc.

(1) Where a guardianship application, duly made under the provisions of this Part of this Act and forwarded to the local social services authority within the period allowed by subsection (2) below is accepted by that authority, the application shall, subject to regulations made by the Secretary of State, confer on the authority or person named in the application as guardian, to the exclusion of any other person—

(a) the power to require the patient to reside at a place specified by the authority or person named as guardian ;

(b) the power to require the patient to attend at places and times so specified for the purpose of medical treatment, occupation, education or training;

(c) the power to require access to the patient to be given, at any place where the patient is residing, to any registered medical practitioner, approved social worker or other person so specified.

(2) The period within which a guardianship application is required for the purposes of this section to be forwarded to the local social services authority is the period of 14 days beginning with the date on which the patient was last examined by a registered medical practitioner before giving a medical recommendation for the purposes of the application.

(3) A guardianship application which appears to be duly made and to be founded on the necessary medical recommendations may be acted upon without further proof of the signature or qualification of the person by whom the application or any such medical recommendation is made or given, or of any matter of fact or opinion stated in the application.

(4) If within the period of 14 days beginning with the day on which a guardianship application has been accepted by the local social services authority the application, or any medical recommendation given for the purposes of the application, is found to be in any respect incorrect or defective, the application or recommendation may, within that period and with the consent of that authority, be amended by the person by whom it was signed; and upon such amendment being made the application or recommendation shall have effect and shall be deemed to have had effect as if it had been originally made as so amended.

(5) Where a patient is received into guardianship in pursuance of a guardianship application, any previous application under this Part of this Act by virtue of which he was subject to guardianship or liable to be detained in a hospital shall cease to have effect.

### 9 Regulations as to guardianship

(1) Subject to the provisions of this Part of this Act, the Secretary of State may make regulations—

(a) for regulating the exercise by the guardians of patients received into guardianship under this Part of this Act of their powers as such ; and

(b) for imposing on such guardians, and upon local social services authorities in the case of patients under the guardianship of persons other than local social services authorities, such duties as he considers necessary or expedient in the interests of the patients.

(2) Regulations under this section may in particular make provision for requiring the patients to be visited, on such occasions or at such intervals as may be prescribed by the regulations, on behalf of such local social services authorities as may be so prescribed, and shall provide for the appointment, in the case of every patient subject to the guardianship of a person other than a local social services authority, of a registered medical practitioner to act as the nominated medical attendant of the patient.

### 10 Transfer of guardianship in case of death, incapacity, etc., of guardian

(1) If any person (other than a local social services authority) who is the guardian of a patient received into guardianship under this Part of this Act—

(a) dies; or

(b) gives notice in writing to the local social services authority that he desires to relinquish the functions of guardian,

the guardianship of the patient shall thereupon vest in the local social services authority, but without prejudice to any power to transfer the patient into the guardianship of another person in pursuance of regulations under section 19 below.

(2) If any such person, not having given notice under subsection (1)(b) above, is incapacitated by illness or any other cause from performing the functions of guardian of the patient, those functions may, during his incapacity, be performed on his behalf by the local social services authority or by any other person approved for the purposes by that authority.

(3) If it appears to the county court, upon application made by an approved social worker, that any person other than a local social services authority having the guardianship of a patient received into guardianship under this Part of this Act has performed his functions negligently or in a manner contrary to the interests of the welfare of the patient, the court may order that the guardianship of the patient be transferred to the local social services authority or to any other person approved for the purpose by that authority.

(4) Where the guardianship of a patient is transferred to a local social services authority or other person by or under this section, subsection (2)(c) of section 19 below shall apply as if the patient had been transferred into the guardianship of that authority or person in pursuance of regulations under that section.

*General provisions as to applications and recommendations*

## 11 General provisions as to applications

(1) Subject to the provisions of this section, an application for admission for assessment, an application for admission for treatment and a guardianship application may be made either by the nearest relative of the patient or by an approved social worker; and every such application shall specify die qualification of the applicant to make the application.

(2) Every application for admission shall be addressed to the managers of the hospital to which admission is sought and every guardianship application shall be forwarded to the local social services authority named in the application as guardian, or, as the case may be, to the local social services authority for the area in which the person so named resides.

(3) Before or within a reasonable time after an application for the admission of a patient for assessment is made by an approved social worker, that social worker shall take such steps as are practicable to inform the person (if any) appearing to be the nearest relative of the patient that the application is to be or has been made and of the power of the nearest relative under section 23(2)(a) below.

(4) Neither an application for admission for treatment nor a guardianship application shall be made by an approved social worker if the nearest relative of the patient has notified that social worker, or the local social services authority by whom that social worker is appointcd, that hc objects to the application being made and, without prejudice to the foregoing provision, no such application shall be made by such a social worker except after consultation with the person (if any) appearing to be the nearest relative of the patient unless it appears to that social worker that in the circumstances such consultation is not reasonably practicable or would involve unreasonable delay.

(5) None of the applications mentioned in subsection (1) above shall be made by any person in respect of a patient unless that person has personally seen the patient within the period of 14 days ending with the date of the application.

(6) An application for admission for treatment or a guardianship application, and any recommendation given for the purposes of such an application, may describe the patient as suffering from more than one of the following forms of mental disorder, namely mental illness, severe mental impairment, psychopathic disorder or mental impairment; but the application shall be of no effect unless the patient is described in each of the recommendations as suffering from the same form of mental disorder, whether or not he is also described in either of those recommendations as suffering from another form.

(7) Each of the applications mentioned in subsection (1) above shall be sufficient if the recommendations on which it is founded are given either as separate recommendations, each signed by a registered medical practitioner, or as a joint recommendation signed by two such practitioners.

## 12 General provisions as to medical recommendations

(1) The recommendations required for the purposes of an application for the admission of a patient under this Part of this Act (in this Act referred to as " medical recommendations ") shall be signed on or before the date of the application, and shall be given by practitioners who have personally examined the patient either together or

separately, but where they have examined the patient separately not more than five days must have elapsed between the days on which the separate examinations took place.

(2) Of the medical recommendations given for the purposes of any such application, one shall be given by a practitioner approved for the purposes of this section by title Secretary of State as having special experience in the diagnosis or treatment of mental disorder; and unless that practitioner has previous acquaintance with the patient, the other such recommendation shall, if practicable, be given by a registered medical practitioner who has such previous acquaintance.

(3) Subject to subsection (4) below, where the application is for the admission of the patient to a hospital which is not a mental nursing home, one (but not more than one) of the medical recommendations may be given by a practitioner on the staff of that hospital, except where the patient is proposed to be accommodated under section 65 or 66 of the National Health Service Act 1977 (which relate to accommodation for private patients).

(4) Subsection (3) above shall not preclude both the medical recommendations being given by practitioners on the staff of the hospital in question if—

- (a) compliance with that subsection would result in delay involving serious risk to the health or safety of the patient; and
- (b) one of the practitioners giving the recommendations works at the hospital for less than half of the time which he is bound by contract to devote to work in the health service; and
- (c) where one of those practitioners is a consultant, the other does not work (whether at the hospital or elsewhere) in a grade in which he is under that consultant's directions.

(5) A medical recommendation for the purposes of an application for the admission of a patient under this Part of this Act shall not be given by—

- (a) the applicant;
- (b) a partner of the applicant or of a practitioner by whom another medical recommendation is given for the purposes of the same application;
- (c) a person employed as an assistant by the applicant or by any such practitioner;
- (d) a person who receives or has an interest in the receipt of any payments made on account of the maintenance of the patient; or
- (e) except as provided by subsection (3) or (4) above, a practitioner on the staff of the hospital to which the patient is to be admitted,

or by the husband, wife, father, father-in-law, mother, mother-in-law, son, son-in-law, daughter, daughter-in-law, brother, brother-in-law, sister or sister-in-law of the patient, or of any person mentioned in paragraphs (a) to (e) above, or of a practitioner by whom another medical recommendation is given for the purposes of the same application.

(6) A general practitioner who is employed part-time in a hospital shall not for the purposes of this section be regarded as a practitioner on its staff.

(7) Subsections (1), (2) and (5) above shall apply to applications for guardianship as they apply to applications for admission but with the substitution for paragraph (e) of subsection (5) above of the following paragraph—

“(e) the person named as guardian in the application.”.

## 13 Duty of approved social workers to make applications for admission or guardianship

(1) It shall be the duty of an approved social worker to make an application for admission to hospital or a guardianship application in respect of a patient within the area of the local social services authority by which that officer is appointed in any case where he is satisfied that such an application ought to be made and is of the opinion, having regard to any wishes expressed by relatives of the patient or any other relevant circumstances, that it is necessary or proper for the application to be made by him.

(2) Before making an application for the admission of a patient to hospital an approved social worker shall interview the patient in a suitable manner and satisfy himself that detention in a hospital is in all the circumstances of the case the most appropriate way of providing the care and medical treatment of which the patient stands in need.

(3) An application under this section by an approved social worker may be made outside the area of the local social services authority by which he is appointed.

(4) It shall be the duty of a local social services authority, if so required by the nearest relative of a patient residing in their area, to direct an approved social worker as soon as practicable to take the patient's case into consideration under subsection (1) above with a view to making an application for his admission to hospital; and if in any such case that approved social worker decides not to make an application he shall inform the nearest relative of his reasons in writing.

(5) Nothing in this section shall be construed as authorising or requiring an application to be made by an approved social worker in contravention of the provisions of section 11(4) above, or as restricting the power of an approved social worker to make any application under this Act.

## 14 Social reports

Where a patient is admitted to a hospital in pursuance of an application (other than an emergency application) made under this Part of this Act by his nearest relative, the managers of the hospital shall as soon as practicable give notice of that fact to the local social services authority for the area in which the patient resided immediately before his admission; and that authority shall as soon as practicable arrange for a social worker of their social services department to interview the patient and provide the managers with a report on his social circumstances.

## 15 Rectification of applications and recommendations

(1) If within the period of 14 days beginning with the day on which a patient has been admitted to a hospital in pursuance of an application for admission for assessment or for treatment the application, or any medical recommendation given for the purposes of the application, is found to be in any respect incorrect or defective, the application or recommendation may, within that period and with the consent of the managers of the hospital, be amended by the person by whom it was signed; and upon such amendment being made the application or recommendation shall have effect and shall be deemed to have had effect as if it had been originally made as so amended.

(2) Without prejudice to subsection (1) above, if within the period mentioned in that subsection it appears to the managers of the hospital that one of the two medical recommendations on which an application for the admission of a patient is founded is

insufficient to warrant the detention of the patient in pursuance of the application, they may, within that period, give notice in writing to that effect to the applicant; and where any such notice is given in respect of a medical recommendation, that recommendation shall be disregarded, but the application shall be, and shall be deemed always to have been, sufficient if—

(a) a fresh medical recommendation complying with the relevant provisions of this Part of this Act (other than the provisions relating to the time of signature and the interval between examinations) is furnished to the managers within that period ; and

(b) that recommendation, and the other recommendation on which the application is founded, together comply with those provisions.

(3) Where the medical recommendations upon which an aplication for admission is founded are, taken together, insufficient to warrant the detention of the patient in pursuance of the application, a notice under subsection (2) above may be given in respect of either of those recommendations; but this subsection shall not apply in a case where the application is of no effect by virtue of section 11(6) above.

(4) Nothing in this section shall be construed as authorising the giving of notice in respect of an application made as an emergency application, or the detention of a patient admitted in pursuance of such an application, after the period of 72 hours referred to in section 4(4) above, unless the conditions set out in paragraphs (a) and (b) of that section are complied with or would be complied with apart from any error or defect to which this section applies.

*Position of patients subject to detention or guardianship*

## 16 Reclassification of patients

(1) If in the case of a patient who is for the time being detained in a hospital in pursuance of an application for admission for treatment, or subject to guardianship in pursuance of a guardianship application, it appears to the appropriate medical officer that the patient is suffering from a form of mental disorder other than the form or forms specified in the application, he may furnish to the managers of the hospital, or to the guardian, as the case may be, a report to that effect; and where a report is so furnished, the application shall have effect as if that other form of mental disorder were specified in it.

(2) Where a report under subsection (1) above in respect of a patient detained in a hospital is to the effect that he is suffering from psychopathic disorder or mental impairment but not from mental illness or severe mental impairment the appropriate medical officer shall include in the report a statement of his opinion whether further medical treatment in hospital is likely to alleviate or prevent a deterioration of the patient's condition ; and if he states that in his opinion such treatment is not likely to have that effect the authority of the managers to detain the patient shall cease.

(3) Before furnishing a report under subsection (1) above the appropriate medical officer shall consult one or more other persons who have been professionally concerned with the patient's medical treatment.

(4) Where a report is furnished under this section in respect of a patient, the managers or guardian shall cause the patient and the nearest relative to be informed.

(5) In this section " appropriate medical officer " means—

(a) in the case of a patient who is subject to the guardianship of a person other than a local social services authority, the nominated medical attendant of the patient; and

(b) in any other case, the responsible medical officer.

## 17 Leave of absence from hospital

(1) The responsible medical officer may grant to any patient who is for the time being liable to be detained in a hospital under this Part of this Act leave to be absent from the hospital subject to such conditions (if any) as that officer considers necessary in the interests of the patient or for the protection of other persons.

(2) Leave of absence may be granted to a patient under this section either indefinitely or on specified occasions or for any specified period; and where leave is so granted for a specified period, that period may be extended by further leave granted in the absence of the patient.

(3) Where it appears to the responsible medical officer that it is necessary so to do in the interests of the patient or for the protection of other persons, he may, upon granting leave of absence under this section, direct that the patient remain in custody during his absence; and where leave of absence is so granted the patient may be kept in the custody of any officer on the staff of the hospital, or of any other person authorised in writing by the managers of the hospital or, if the patient is required in accordance with conditions imposed on the grant of leave of absence to reside in another hospital, of any officer on the staff of that other hospital.

(4) In any case where a patient is absent from a hospital in pursuance of leave of absence granted under this section, and it appears to the responsible medical officer that it is necessary so to do in the interests of the patient's health or safety or for the protection of other persons, that officer may, subject to subsection (5) below, by notice in writing given to the patient or to the person for the time being in charge of the patient, revoke the leave of absence and recall the patient to the hospital.

(5) A patient to whom leave of absence is granted under this section shall not be recalled under subsection (4) above after he has ceased to be liable to be detained under this Part of this Act; and without prejudice to any other provision of this Part of this Act any such patient shall cease to be so liable at the expiration of the period of six months beginning with the first day of his absence on leave unless either—

(a) he has returned to the hospital, or has been transferred to another hospital under the following provisions of this Act, before the expiration of that period; or

(b) he is absent without leave at the expiration of that period.

## 18 Return and readmission of patients absent without leave

(1) Where a patient who is for the time being liable to be detained under this Part of this Act in a hospital—

(a) absents himself from the hospital without leave granted under section 17 above; or

(b) fails to return to the hospital on any occasion on which, or at the expiration of any period for which, leave of absence was granted to him under that section, or upon being recalled under that section; or

(c) absents himself without permission from any place where he is required to reside in accordance with conditions imposed on the grant of leave of absence under that section,

he may, subject to the provisions of this section, be taken into custody and returned to the hospital or place by any approved social worker, by any officer on the staff of the hospital, by any constable, or by any person authorised in writing by the managers of the hospital.

(2) Where the place referred to in paragraph (c) of subsection (1) above is a hospital other than the one in which the patient is for the time being liable to be detained, the references in that subsection to an officer on the staff of the hospital and the managers of the hospital shall respectively include references to an officer on the staff of the first-mentioned hospital and the managers of that hospital.

(3) Where a patient who is for the time being subject to guardianship under this Part of this Act absents himself without the leave of the guardian from the place at which he is required by the guardian to reside, he may, subject to the provisions of this section, be taken into custody and returned to that place by any officer on the staff of a local social services authority, by any constable, or by any person authorised in writing by the guardian or a local social services authority.

(4) A patient shall not be taken into custody under this section after the expiration of the period of 28 days beginning with the first day of his absence without leave; and a patient who has not returned or been taken into custody under this section within the said period shall cease to be liable to be detained or subject to guardianship, as the case may be, at the expiration of that period.

(5) A patient shall not be taken into custody under this section if the period for which he is liable to be detained is that specified in section 2(4), 4(4) or 5(2) or (4) above and that period has expired.

(6) In this Act " absent without leave " means absent from any hospital or other place and liable to be taken into custody and returned under this section, and related expressions shall be construed accordingly.

## 19 Regulations as to transfer of patients

(1) In such circumstances and subject to such conditions as may be prescribed by regulations made by the Secretary of State

(a) a patient who is for the time being liable to be detained in a hospital by virtue of an application under this Part of this Act may be transferred to another hospital or into the guardianship of a local social services authority or of any person approved by such an authority;

(b) a patient who is for the time being subject to the guardianship of a local social services authority or other person by virtue of an application under this Part of this Act may be transferred into the guardianship of another local social services authority or person, or be transferred to a hospital.

(2) Where a patient is transferred in pursuance of regulations under this section, the provisions of this Part of this Act (including this subsection) shall apply to him as follows, that is to say—

(a) in the case of a patient who is liable to be detained in a hospital by virtue of an application for admission for assessment or for treatment and is transferred to another hospital, as if the application were an application for admission to that other hospital and as if the patient had been admitted to that other hospital at the time when he was originally admitted in pursuance of the application;

(b) in the case of a patient who is liable to be detained in a hospital by virtue of such an application and is transferred into guardianship, as if the application were a guardianship application duly accepted at the said time;

(c) in the case of a patient who is subject to guardianship by virtue of a guardianship application and is transferred into the guardianship of another authority or person, as if the application were for his reception into the guardianship of that authority or person and had been accepted at the time when it was originally accepted;

(d) in the case of a patient who is subject to guardianship by virtue of a guardianship application and is transferred to a hospital, as if the guardianship application were an application for admission to that hospital for treatment and as if the patient had been admitted to the hospital at the time when the application was originally accepted.

(3) Without prejudice to subsections (1) and (2) above, any patient, who is for the time being liable to be detained under this Part of this Act in a hospital vested in the Secretary of State for the purposes of his functions under the National Health Service Act 1977 or any accommodation used under Part I of that Act by the managers of such a hospital, may at any time be removed to any other such hospital or accommodation for which the managers of the first-mentioned hospital are also the managers ; and paragraph (a) of subsection (2) above shall apply in relation to a patient so removed as it applies in relation to a patient transferred in pursuance of regulations made under this section.

(4) Regulations made under this section may make provision for regulating the conveyance to their destination of patients authorised to be transferred or removed in pursuance of the regulations or under subsection (3) above.

*Duration of detention or guardianship and discharge*

## 20 Duration of authority

(1) Subject to the following provisions of this Part of this Act, a patient admitted to hospital in pursuance of an application for admission for treatment, and a patient placed under guardianship in pursuance of a guardianship application, may be detained in a hospital or kept under guardianship for a period not exceeding six months beginning with the day on which he was so admitted, or the day on which the guardianship application was accepted, as the case may be, but shall not be so detained or kept for any longer period unless the authority for his detention or guardianship is renewed under this section.

(2) Authority for the detention or guardianship of a patient may, unless the patient has previously been discharged, be renewed—

(a) from the expiration of the period referred to in subsection (1) above, for a further period of six months;

(b) from the expiration of any period of renewal under paragraph (a) above, for a further period of one year,

and so on for periods of one year at a time.

(3) Within the period of two months ending on the day on which a patient who is liable to be detained in pursuance of an application for admission for treatment would cease under this section to be so liable in default of the renewal of the authority for his detention, it shall be the duty of the responsible medical officer—

(a) to examine the patient; and

(b) if it appears to him that the conditions set out in subsection (4) below are satisfied, to furnish to the managers of the hospital where the patient is detained a report to that effect in the prescribed form ;

and where such a report is furnished in respect of a patient the managers shall, unless they discharge the patient, cause him to be informed.

(4) The conditions referred to in subsection (3) above are that—

(a) the patient is suffering from mental illness, severe mental impairment, psychopathic disorder or mental impairment, and his mental disorder is of a nature or degree which makes it appropriate for him to receive medical treatment in a hospital; and

(b) such treatment is likely to alleviate or prevent a deterioration of his condition; and

(c) it is necessary for the health or safety of the patient or for the protection of other persons that he should receive such treatment and that it cannot be provided unless he continues to be detained ;

but, in the case of mental illness or severe mental impairment, it shall be an alternative to the condition specified in paragraph (b) above that the patient, if discharged, is unlikely to be able to care for himself, to obtain the care which he needs or to guard himself against serious exploitation.

(5) Before furnishing a report under subsection (3) above the responsible medical officer shall consult one or more other persons who have been professionally concerned with the patient's medical treatment

(6) Within the period of two months ending with the day on which a patient who is subject to guardianship under this Part of this Act would cease under this section to be so liable in default of the renewal of the authority for his guardianship, it shall be the duty of the appropriate medical officer—

(a) to examine the patient; and

(b) if it appears to him that the conditions set out in subsection (7) below are satisfied, to furnish to the guardian and, where the guardian is a person other than a local social services authority, to the responsible local social services authority a report to that effect in the prescribed form ;

and where such a report is furnished in respect of a patient, the local social services authority shall, unless they discharge the patient, cause him to be informed.

(7) The conditions referred to in subsection (6) above are that—

(a) the patient is suffering from mental illness, severe mental impairment, psychopathic disorder or mental impairment and his mental disorder is of a nature or degree which warrants his reception into guardianship ; and

(b) it is necessary in the interests of the welfare of the patient or for the protection of other persons that the patient should remain under guardianship.

(8) Where a report is duly furnished under subsection (3) or (6) above, the authority for the detention or guardianship of the patient shall be thereby renewed for the period prescribed in that case by subsection (2) above.

(9) Where the form of mental disorder specified in a report furnished under subsection (3) or (6) above is a form of disorder other than that specified in the application for admission for treatment or, as the case may be, in the guardianship application, that application shall have effect as if that other form of mental disorder were specified in it; and where on any occasion a report specifying such a form of mental disorder is furnished under either of those subsections the appropriate medical officer need not on that occasion furnish a report under section 16 above.

(10) In this section " appropriate medical officer" has the same meaning as in section 16(5) above.

### 21 Special provisions as to patients absent without leave

(1) If on the day on which, apart from this section, a patient would cease to be liable to be detained or subject to guardianship under this Part of this Act or, within the period of one week ending with that day, the patient is absent without leave, he shall not cease to be so liable or subject—

- (a) in any case, until the expiration of the period during which he can be taken into custody under section 18 above or the day on which he is returned or returns himself to the hospital or place where he ought to be, whichever is the earlier ; and
- (b) if he is so returned or so returns himself within the period first mentioned in paragraph (a) above, until the expiration of the period of one week beginning with thc day on which he is so returned or so returns.

(2) Where the period for which a patient is liable to be detained or subject to guardianship is extended by virtue of this section, any examination and report to be made and furnished under section 20(3) or (6) above may be made and furnished within that period as so extended.

(3) Where the authority for the detention or guardianship of a patient is renewed by virtue of this section after the day on which, apart from this section, that authority would have expired under section 20 above, the renewal shall take effect as from that day.

### 22 Special provisions as to patients sentenced to imprisonment, etc.

(1) Where a patient who is liable to be detained by virtue of an application for admission for treatment or is subject to guardianship by virtue of a guardianship application is detained in custody in pursuance of any sentence or order passed or made by a court in the United Kingdom (including an order committing or remanding him in custody), and is so detained for a period exceeding, or for successive periods exceeding in the aggregate, six months, the application shall cease to have effect at the expiration of that period.

(2) Where any such patient is so detained in custody but the application does not cease to have effect under subsection (1) above, then—

- (a) if apart from this subsection the patient would have ceased to be liable to be so detained or subject to guardianship on or before the day on which he is discharged from custody, he shall not cease and shall be deemed not to have ceased to be so liable or subject until the end of that day ; and
- (b) in any case, sections 18 and 21 above shall apply in relation to the patient as if he had absented himself without leave on that day.

## 23 Discharge of patients

(1) Subject to the provisions of this section and section 25 below, a patient who is for the time being liable to be detained or subject to guardianship under this Part of this Act shall cease to be so liable or subject if an order in writing discharging him from detention or guardianship (in this Act referred to as " an order for discharge ") is made in accordance with this section.

(2) An order for discharge may be made in respect of a patient—

(a) where the patient is liable to be detained in a hospital in pursuance of an application for admission for assessmeat or for treatment by the responsible medical officer, by the managers or by the nearest relative of the patient;

(b) where the patient is subject to guardianship, by the responsible medical officer, by the responsible local social services authority or by the nearest relative of the patient.

(3) Where the patient is liable to be detained in a mental nursing home in pursuance of an application for admission for assessment or for treatment, an order for his discharge may, without prejudice to subsection (2) above, be made by the Secretary of State and, if the patient is maintained under a contract with a Regional Health Authority, District Health Authority or special health authority, by that authority.

(4) The powers conferred by this section on any authority or body of persons may be exercised by any three or more members of that authority or body authorised by them in that behalf or by three or more members of a committee or subcommittee of that authority or body which has been authorised by them in that behalf.

## 24 Visiting and examination of patients

(1) For the purpose of advising as to the exercise by the nearest relative of a patient who is liable to be detained or subject to guardianship under this Part of this Act of any power to order his discharge, any registered medical practitioner authorised by or on behalf of the nearest relative of the patient may, at any reasonable time, visit the patient and examine him in private.

(2) Any registered medical practitioner authorised for the purposes of subsection (1) above to visit and examine a patient may require the production of and inspect any records relating to the detention or treatment of the patient in any hospital.

(3) Where application is made by the Secretary of State or a Regional Health Authority, District Health Authority or special health authority to exercise, in respect of a patient liable to be detained in a mental nursing home, any power to make an order for his discharge, the following persons, that is to say—

(a) any registered medical practitioner authorised by the Secretary of State or, as the case may be, that authority; and

(b) any other person (whether a registered medical practitioner or not) authorised under the Nursing Homes Act 1975 to inspect the home,

may at any reasonable time visit the patient and interview him in private.

(4) Any person authorised for the purposes of subsection (3) above to visit a patient may require the production of and inspect any documents constituting or alleged to constitute the authority for the detention of the patient under this Part of this Act; and any person so authorised, who is a registered medical practitioner, may examine the

patient in private, and may require the production of and inspect any other records relating to the treatment of the patient in the home.

## 25 Restrictions on discharge by nearest relative

(1) An order for the discharge of a patient who is liable to be detained in a hospital shall not be made by his nearest relative except after giving not less than 72 hours' notice in writing to the managers of the hospital; and if, within 72 hours after such notice has been given, the responsible medical officer furnishes to the managers a report certifying that in the opinion of that officer the patient, if discharged, would be likely to act in a manner dangerous to other persons or to himself—

(a) any order for the discharge of the patient made by that relative in pursuance of the notice shall be of no effect; and

(b) no further order for the discharge of the patient shall be made by that relative during the period of six months beginning with the date of the report.

(2) In any case where a report under subsection (1) above is furnished in respect of a patient who is liable to be detained in pursuance of an application for admission for treatment the managers shall cause the nearest relative of the patient to be informed.

*Functions of relatives of patients*

## 26 Definition of " relative " and " nearest relative "

(1) In this Part of this Act " relative " means any of the following persons:—

(a) husband or wife;

(b) son or daughter;

(c) father or mother;

(d) brother or sister;

(e) grandparent;

(f) grandchild;

(g) uncle or aunt;

(h) nephew or niece.

(2) In deducing relationships for the purposes of this section, any relationship of the half-blood shall be treated as a relationship of the whole blood, and an illegitimate person shall be treated as the legitimate child of his mother.

(3) In this Part of this Act, subject to the provisions of this section and to the following provisions of this Part of this Act, the " nearest relative " means the person first described in subsection (1) above who is for the time being surviving, relatives of the whole blood being preferred to relatives of the same description of the half-blood and the elder or eldest of two or more relatives described in any paragraph of that subsection being preferred to the other or others of those relatives, regardless of sex.

(4) Subject to the provisions of this section and to the following provisions of this Part of this Act, where the patient ordinarily resides with or is cared for by one or more of his relatives (or, if he is for the time being an in-patient in a hospital, he last ordinarily resided with or was cared for by one or more of his relatives) his nearest relative shall be determined—

(a) by giving preference to that relative or those relatives over the other or others ; and

(b) as between two or more such relatives, in accordance with subsection (3) above.

(5) Where the person who, under subsection (3) or (4) above, would be the nearest relative of a patient—

(a) in the case of a patient ordinarily resident in the United Kingdom, the Channel Islands or the Isle of Man, is not so resident; or

(b) is the husband or wife of the patient, but is permanently separated from the patient, either by agreement or under an order of a court, or has deserted or has been deserted by the patient for a period which has not come to an end ; or

(c) is a person other than the husband, wife, father or mother of the patient, and is for the time being under 18 years of age ; or

(d) is a person against whom an order divesting him of authority over the patient has been made under section 38 of the Sexual Offences Act 1956 (which relates to incest with a person under eighteen) and has not been rescinded,

the nearest relative of the patient shall be ascertained as if that person were dead.

(6) In this section " husband " and " wife " include a person who is living with the patient as the patient's husband or wife, as the case may be (or, if the patient is for the time being an in-patient in a hospital, was so living until the patient was admitted), and has been or had been so living for a period of not less than six months; but a person shall not be treated by virtue of this subsection as the nearest relative of a married patient unless the husband or wife of the patient is disregarded by virtue of paragraph (b) of subsection (5) above.

(7) A person, other than a relative, with whom the patient ordinarily resides (or, if the patient is for the time being an inpatient in a hospital, last ordinarily resided before he was admitted), and with whom he has or had been ordinarily residing for a period of not less than five years, shall be treated for the purposes of this Part of this Act as if he were a relative but—

(a) shall be treated for the purposes of subsection (3) above as if mentioned last in subsection (1) above; and

(b) shall not be treated by virtue of this subsection as the nearest relative of a married patient unless the husband or wife of the patient is disregarded by virtue of paragraph (b) of subsection (5) above.

## 27 Children and young persons in care of local authority

In any case where the rights and powers of a parent of a patient, being a child or young person, are vested in a local authority or other person by virtue of—

(a) section 3 of the Child Care Act 1980 (which relates to the assumption by a local authority of parental rights and duties in relation to a child in their care);

(b) section 10 of that Act (which relates to the powers and duties of local authorities with respect to persons committed to their care under the Children and Young Persons Act 1969); or

(c) section 17 of the Social Work (Scotland) Act 1968 (which makes corresponding provision for Scotland),

that authority or person shall be deemed to be the nearest relative of the patient in preference to any person except the patient's husband or wife (if any) and except, in a case where the said rights and powers are vested in a local authority by virtue of subsection (1) of the said section 3, any parent of the patient not being the person on whose account the resolution mentioned in that subsection was passed.

## 28 Nearest relative of minor under guardianship, etc.

(1) Where a patient who has not attained the age of 18 years—

(a) is, by virtue of an order made by a court in the exercise of jurisdiction (whether under any enactment or otherwise) in respect of the guardianship of minors (including an order under section 38 of the Sexual Offences Act 1956), or by virtue of a deed or will executed by his father or mother, under the guardianship of a person who is not his nearest relative under the foregoing provisions of this Act, or is under the joint guardianship of two persons of whom one is such a person; or

(b) is, by virtue of an order made by a court in the exercise of such jurisdiction or in matrimonial proceedings, or by virtue of a separation agreement between his father and mother, in the custody of any such person,

the person or persons having the guardianship or custody of the patient shall, to the exclusion of any other person, be deemed to be his nearest relative.

(2) Subsection (5) of section 26 above shall apply in relation to a person who is, or who is one of the persons, deemed to be the nearest relative of a patient by virtue of this section as it applies in relation to a person who would be the nearest relative under subsection (3) of that section.

(3) A patient shall be treated for the purposes of this section as being in the custody of another person if he would be in that other person's custody apart from section 8 above.

(4) In this section " court" includes a court in Scotland or Northern Ireland, and " enactment" includes an enactment of the Parliament of Northern Ireland, a Measure of the Northern Ireland Assembly and an Order in Council under Schedule 1 of the Northern Ireland Act 1974.

## 29 Appointment by court of acting nearest relative

(1) The county court may, upon application made in accordance with the provisions of this section in respect of a patient, by order direct that the functions of the nearest relative of the patient under this Part of this Act and sections 66 and 69 below shall, during the continuance in force of the order, be exercisable by the applicant, or by any other person specified in the application, being a person who, in the opinion of the court, is a proper person to act as the patient's nearest relative and is willing to do so.

(2) An order under this section may be made on the application of—

(a) any relative of the patient;

(b) any other person with whom the patient is residing (or, if the patient is then an in-patient in a hospital, was last residing before he was admitted); or

(c) an approved social worker ;

but in relation to an application made by such a social worker, subsection (1) above shall have effect as if for the words " the applicant" there were substituted the words " the local social services authority " .

(3) An application for an order under this section may be made upon any of the following grounds, that is to say—

(a) that the patient has no nearest relative within the meaning of this Act, or that it is not reasonably practicable to ascertain whether he has such a relative, or who that relative is;

(b) that the nearest relative of the patient is incapable of acting as such by reason of mental disorder or other illness;

(c) that the nearest relative of the patient unreasonably objects to the making of an application for admission for treatment or a guardianship application in respect of the patient; or

(d) that the nearest relative of the patient has exercised without due regard to the welfare of the patient or the interests of the public his power to discharge the patient from hospital or guardianship under this Part of this Act, or is likely to do so.

(4) If, immediately before the expiration of the period for which a patient is liable to be detained by virtue of an application for admission for assessment, an application under this section, which is an application made on the ground specified in subsection (3)(c) or (d) above, is pending in respect of the patient, that period shall be extended—

(a) in any case, until the application under this section has been finally disposed of ; and

(b) if an order is made in pursuance of the application under this section, for a further period of seven days;

and for the purposes of this subsection an application under this section shall be deemed to have been finally disposed of at the expiration of the time allowed for appealing from the decision of the court or, if notice of appeal has been given within that time, when the appeal has been heard or withdrawn, and " pending " shall be construed accordingly.

(5) An order made on the ground specified in subsection (3)(a) or (b) above may specify a period for which it is to continue in force unless previously discharged under section 30 below.

(6) While an order made under this section is in force, the provisions of this Part of this Act (other than this section and section 30 below) and sections 66, 69, 132(4) and 133 below shall apply in relation to the patient as if for any reference to the nearest relative of the patient there were substituted a reference to the person having the functions of that relative and (without prejudice to section 30 below) shall so apply notwithstanding that the person who was the patient's nearest relative when the order was made is no longer his nearest relative; but this subsection shall not apply to section 66 below in the case mentioned in paragraph (h) of subsection (1) of that section.

### 30 Discharge and variation of orders under s. 29

(1) An order made under section 29 above in respect of a patient may be discharged by the county court upon application made—

(a) in any case, by the person having the functions of the nearest relative of the patient by virtue of the order;

(b) where the order was made on the ground specified in paragraph (a) or paragraph (b) of section 29(3) above, or where the person who was the nearest relative of the patient when the order was made has ceased to be his nearest relative, on the application of the nearest relative of the patient.

(2) An order made under section 29 above in respect of a patient may be varied by the county court, on the application of the person having the functions of the nearest relative by virtue of the order or on the application of an approved social worker, by substituting for the first-mentioned person a local social services authority or any other person who in the opinion of the court is a proper person to exercise those functions, being an authority or person who is willing to do so.

(3) If the person having the functions of the nearest relative of a patient by virtue of an order under section 29 above dies—

(a) subsections (1) and (2) above shall apply as if for any reference to that person there were substituted a reference to any relative of the patient, and

(b) until the order is discharged or varied under those provisions the functions of the nearest relative under this Part of this Act and sections 66 and 69 below shall not be exercisable by any person.

(4) An order under section 29 above shall, unless previously discharged under subsection (1) above, cease to have effect at the expiration of the period, if any, specified under subsection (5) of that section or, where no such period is specified—

(a) if the patient was on the date of the order liable to be detained in pursuance of an application for admission for treatment or by virtue of an order or direction under Part III of this Act (otherwise than under section 35, 36 or 38) or was subject to guardianship under this Part of this Act or by virtue of such an order or direction, or becomes so liable or subject within the period of three months beginning with that date, when he ceases to be so liable or subject (otherwise than on being transferred in pursuance of regulations under section 19 above);

(b) if the patient was not on the date of the order, and has not within the said period become, so liable or subject, at the expiration of that period.

(5) The discharge or variation under this section of an order made under section 29 above shall not affect the validity of anything previously done in pursuance of the order.

*Supplemental*

## 31 Procedure on applications to county court

County court rules which relate to applications authorised by this Part of this Act to be made to a county court may make provision—

(a) for the hearing and determination of such applications otherwise than in open court;

(b) for the admission on the hearing of such applications of evidence of such descriptions as may be specified in the rules notwithstanding anything to the contrary in any enactment or rule of law relating to the admissibility of evidence;

(c) for the visiting and interviewing of patients in private by or under the directions of the court.

## 32 Regulations for purposes of Part II

(1) The Secretary of State may make regulations for prescribing anything which, under this Part of this Act, is required or authorised to be prescribed, and otherwise for carrying this Part of this Act into full effect.

(2) Regulations under this section may in particular make provision—

(a) for prescribing the form of any application, recommendation, report, order, notice or other document to be made or given under this Part of this Act;

(b) for prescribing the manner in which any such application, recommendation, report, order, notice or other document may be proved, and for regulating the service of any such application, report, order or notice;

(c) for requiring the managers of hospitals and local social services authorities to keep such registers or other records as may be prescribed by the regulations in respect of patients liable to be detained or subject to guardianship under this Part of this Act, and to furnish or make available to those patients, and their relatives, such written statements of their rights and powers under this Act as may be so prescribed;

(d) for the determination in accordance with the regulations of the age of any person whose exact age cannot be ascertained by reference to the registers kept under the Births and Deaths Registration Act 1953 ; and

(e) for enabling the functions under this Part of this Act of the nearest relative of a patient to be performed, in such circumstances and subject to such conditions (if any) as may be prescribed by the regulations, by any person authorised in that behalf by that relative;

and for the purposes of this Part of this Act any application, report or notice the service of which is regulated under paragraph (b) above shall be deemed to have been received by or furnished to the authority or person to whom it is authorised or required to be furnished, addressed or given if it is duly served in accordance with the regulations.

(3) Without prejudice to subsections (1) and (2) above, but subject to section 23(4) above, regulations under this section may determine the manner in which functions under this Part of this Act of the managers of hospitals, local social services authorities, Regional Health Authorities, District Health Authorities or special health authorities are to be exercised, and such regulations may in particular specify the circumstances in which, and the conditions subject to which, any such functions may be performed by officers of or other persons acting on behalf of those managers and authorities.

## 33 Special provisions as to wards of court

(1) An application for the admission to hospital of a minor who is a ward of court may be made under this Part of this Act with the leave of the court; and section 11(4) above shall not apply in relation to an application so made.

(2) Where a minor who is a ward of court is liable to be detained in a hospital by virtue of an application for admission under this Part of this Act, any power exercisable under this Part of this Act or under section 66 below in relation to the patient by his nearest relative shall be exercisable by or with the leave of the court.

(3) Nothing in this Part of this Act shall be construed as authorising the making of a guardianship application in respect of a minor who is a ward of court, or the transfer into guardianship of any such minor.

## 34 Interpretation of Part II

(1) In this Part of this Act—

" the nominated medical attendant", in relation to a patient who is subject to the guardianship of a person other than a local social services authority, means the person appointed in pursuance of regulations made under section 9(2) above to act as the medical attendant of the patient;

" the responsible medical officer " means—

(a) in relation to a patient liable to be detained by virtue of an application for admission for assess-merit or an application for admission for treatment, the registered medical practitioner in charge of the treatment of the patient;

(b) in relation to a patient subject to guardianship, the medical officer authorised by the local social services authority to act (either generally or in any particular case or for any particular purpose) as the responsible medical officer.

(2) Except where otherwise expressly provided, this Part of this Act applies in relation to a mental nursing home, being a home in respect of which the particulars of registration are for the time being entered in the separate part of the register kept for the purposes of section 3 (4)(b) of the Nursing Homes Act 1975, as it applies in relation to a hospital, and references in this Part of this Act to a hospital, and any reference in this Act to a hospital to which this Part of this Act applies, shall be construed accordingly.

(3) In relation to a patient who is subject to guardianship in pursuance of a guardianship application, any reference in this Part of this Act to the responsible local social services authority is a reference—

(a) where the patient is subject to the guardianship of a local social services authority, to that authority ;

(b) where the patient is subject to the guardianship of a person other than a local social services authority, to the local social services authority for the area in which that person resides.

## PART III

### Patients Concerned in Criminal Proceedings or Under Sentence

*Remands to hospital*

#### 35 Remand to hospital for report on accused's mental condition

(1) Subject to the provisions of this section, the Crown Court or a magistrates' court may remand an accused person to a hospital specified by the court for a report on his mental condition.

(2) For the purposes of this section an accused person is—

(a) in relation to the Crown Court, any person who is awaiting trial before the court for an offence punishable with imprisonment or who has been arraigned before the court for such an offence and has not yet been sentenced or otherwise dealt with for the offence on which he has been arraigned ;

(b) in relation to a magistrates' court, any person who has been convicted by the court of an offence punishable on summary conviction with imprisonment and any person charged with such an offence if the court is satisfied that he did the act or made the omission charged or he has consented to the exercise by the court of the powers conferred by this section.

(3) Subject to subsection (4) below, the powers conferred by this section may be exercised if—

(a) the court is satisfied, on the written or oral evidence of a registered medical practitioner, that there is reason to suspect that the accused person is suffering from mental illness, psychopathic disorder, severe mental impairment or mental impairment; and

(b) the court is of the opinion that it would be impracticable for a report on his mental condition to be made if he were remanded on bail;

but those powers shall not be exercised by the Crown Court in respect of a person who has been convicted before the court if the sentence for the offence of which he has been convicted is fixed by law.

(4) The court shall not remand an accused person to a hospital under this section unless satisfied, on the written or oral evidence of the registered medical practitioner who would be responsible for making the report or of some other person representing the managers of the hospital, that arrangements have been made for his admission to that hospital and for his admission to it within the period of seven days beginning with the date of the remand; and if the court is so satisfied it may, pending his admission, give directions for his conveyance to and detention in a place of safety.

(5) Where a court has remanded an accused person under this section it may further remand him if it appears to the court, on the written or oral evidence of the registered medical practitioner responsible for making the report, that a further remand is necessary for completing the assessment of the accused person's mental condition.

(6) The power of further remanding an accused person under this section may be exercised by the court without his being brought before the court if he is represented by counsel or a solicitor and his counsel or solicitor is given an opportunity of being heard.

(7) An accused person shall not be remanded or further remanded under this section for more than 28 days at a time or for more than 12 weeks in all; and the court may at any time terminate the remand if it appears to the court that it is appropriate to do so.

(8) An accused person remanded to hospital under this section shall be entitled to obtain at his own expense an independent report on his mental condition from a registered medical practitioner chosen by him and to apply to the court on the basis of it for his remand to be terminated under subsection (7) above.

(9) Where an accused person is remanded under this section—

(a) a constable or any other person directed to do so by the court shall convey the accused person to the hospital specified by the court within the period mentioned in subsection (4) above ; and

(b) the managers of the hospital shall admit him within that period and thereafter detain him in accordance with the provisions of this section.

(10) If an accused person absconds from a hospital to which he has been remanded under this section, or while being conveyed to or from that hospital, he may be arrested without warrant by any constable and shall, after being arrested, be brought as soon as practicable before the court that remanded him ; and the court may thereupon terminate the remand and deal with him in any way in which it could have dealt with him if he had not been remanded under this section.

### 36 Remand of accused person to hospital for treatment

(1) Subject to the provisions of this section, the Crown Court may, instead of remanding an accused person in custody, remand him to a hospital specified by the court if satisfied, on the written or oral evidence of two registered medical practitioners, that he is suffering from mental illness or severe mental impairment of a nature or degree which makes it appropriate for him to be detained in a hospital for medical treatment.

(2) For the purposes of this section an accused person is any person who is in custody awaiting trial before the Crown Court for an offence punishable with imprisonment (other than an offence the sentence for which is fixed by law) or who at any time before sentence is in custody in the course of a trial before that court for such an offence.

(3) The court shall not remand an accused person under this section to a hospital unless it is satisfied, on the written or oral evidence of the registered medical practitioner who would be in charge of his treatment or of some other person representing the managers of the hospital, that arrangements have been made for his admission to that hospital and for his admission to it within the period of seven days beginning with the date of the remand; and if the court is so satisfied it may, pending his admission, give directions for his conveyance to and detention in a place of safety.

(4) Where a court has remanded an accused person under this section it may further remand him if it appears to the court, on the written or oral evidence of the responsible medical officer, that a further remand is warranted.

(5) The power of further remanding an accused person under this section may be exercised by the court without his being brought before the court if he is represented by counsel or a solicitor and his counsel or solicitor is given an opportunity of being heard.

(6) An accused person shall not be remanded or further remanded under this section for more than 28 days at a time or for more than 12 weeks in all; and the court may at any time terminate the remand if it appears to the court that it is appropriate to do so.

(7) An accused person remanded to hospital under this section shall be entitled to obtain at his own expense an independent report on his mental condition from a registered medical practitioner chosen by him and to apply to the court on the basis of it for his remand to be terminated under subsection (6) above.

(8) Subsections (9) and (10) of section 35 above shall have effect in relation to a remand under this section as they have effect in relation to a remand under that section.

*Hospital and guardianship orders*

### 37 Powers of courts to order hospital admission or guardianship

(1) Where a person is convicted before the Crown Court of an offence punishable with imprisonment other than an offence the sentence for which is fixed by law, or is convicted by a magistrates' court of an offence punishable on summary conviction with imprisonment, and the conditions mentioned in subsection (2) below are satisfied, the court may by order authorise his admission to and detention in such hospital as may be specified in the order or, as the case may be, place him under the guardianship of a local social services authority or of such other person approved by a local social services authority as may be so specified.

(2) The conditions referred to in subsection (1) above are that—

(a) the court is satisfied, on the written or oral evidence of two registered medical practitioners, that the offender is suffering from mental illness, psychopathic disorder, severe mental impairment or mental impairment and that either—
   (i) the mental disorder from which the offender is suffering is of a nature or degree which makes it appropriate for him to be detained in a hospital for medical treatment and, in the case of psychopathic disorder or mental impairment, that such treatment is likely to alleviate or prevent a deterioration of his condition; or
   (ii) in the case of an offender who has attained the age of 16 years, the mental disorder is of a nature or degree which warrants his reception into guardianship under this Act; and

(b) the court is of the opinion, having regard to all the circumstances including the nature of the offence and the character and antecedents of the offender, and to the other available methods of dealing with him, that the most suitable method of disposing of the case is by means of an order under this section.

(3) Where a person is charged before a magistrates' court with any act or omission as an offence and the court would have power, on convicting him of that offence, to make an order under subsection (1) above in his case as being a person suffering from mental illness or severe mental impairment, then, if the court is satisfied that the accused did the act or made the omission charged, the court may, if it thinks fit, make such an order without convicting him.

(4) An order for the admission of an offender to a hospital (in this Act referred to as " a hospital order ") shall not be made under this section unless the court is satisfied on the written or oral evidence of the registered medical practitioner who would be in charge of his treatment or of some other person representing the managers of the hospital that arrangements have been made for his admission to that hospital in the event of such an order being made by the court, and for his admission to it within the period of 28 days beginning with the date of the making of such an order; and the court may, pending his admission within that period, give such directions as it thinks fit for his conveyance to and detention in a place of safety.

(5) If within the said period of 28 days it appears to the Secretary of State that by reason of an emergency or other special circumstances it is not practicable for the patient to be received into the hospital specified in the order, he may give directions for the admission of the patient to such other hospital as appears to be appropriate instead of the hospital so specified ; and where such directions are given—

(a) the Secretary of State shall cause the person having the custody of the patient to be informed, and

(b) the hospital order shall have effect as if the hospital specified in the directions were substituted for the hospital specified in the order.

(6) An order placing an offender under the guardianship of a local social services authority or of any other person (in this Act referred to as " a guardianship order ") shall not be made under this section unless the court is satisfied that that authority or person is willing to receive the offender into guardianship.

(7) A hospital order or guardianship order shall specify the form or forms of mental disorder referred to in subsection (2)(a) above from which, upon the evidence taken into account under that subsection, the offender is found by the court to be sufferring; and no such order shall be made unless the offender is described by each of the practitioners whose evidence is taken into account under that subsection as suffering

from the same one of those forms of mental disorder, whether or not he is also described by either of them as suffering from another of them.

(8) Where an order is made under this section, the court shall not pass sentence of imprisonment or impose a fine or make a probation order in respect of the offence or make any such order as is mentioned in paragraph (b) or (c) of section 7(7) of the Children and Young Persons Act 1969 in respect of the offender, but may make any other order which the court has power to make apart from this section ; and for the purposes of this subsection " sentence of imprisonment" includes any sentence or order for detention.

**38 Interim hospital orders**

(1) Where a person is convicted before the Crown Court of an offence punishable with imprisonment (other than an offence the sentence for which is fixed by law) or is convicted by a magistrates' court of an offence punishable on summary conviction with imprisonment and the court before or by which he is convicted is satisfied, on the written or oral evidence of two registered medical practitioners—

(a) that the offender is suffering from mental illness, psychopathic disorder, severe mental impairment or mental impairment; and

(b) that there is reason to suppose that the mental disorder from which the offender is suffering is such that it may be appropriate for a hospital order to be made in his case,

the court may, before making a hospital order or dealing with him in some other way, make an order (in this Act referred to as " an interim hospital order") authorising his admission to such hospital as may be specified in the order and his detention there in accordance with this section.

(2) In the case of an offender who is subject to an interim hospital order the court may make a hospital order without his being brought before the court if he is represented by counsel or a solicitor and his counsel or solicitor is given an opportunity of being heard.

(3) At least one of the registered medical practitioners whose evidence is taken into account under subsection (1) above shall be employed at the hospital which is to be specified in the order.

(4) An interim hospital order shall not be made for the admission of an offender to a hospital unless the court is satisfied, on the written or oral evidence of the registered medical practitioner who would be in charge of his treatment or of some other person representing the managers of the hospital, that arrangements have been made for his admission to that hospital and for his admission to it within the period of 28 days beginning with the date of the order; and if the court is so satisfied the court may, pending his admission, give directions for his conveyance to and detention in a place of safety.

(5) An interim hospital order—

(a) shall be in force for such period, not exceeding 12 weeks, as the court may specify when making the order; but

(b) may be renewed for further periods of not more than 28 days at a time if it appears to the court, on the written or oral evidence of the responsible medical officer, that the continuation of the order is warranted ;

but no such order shall continue in force for more than six months in all and the court shall terminate the order if it makes a hospital order in respect of the offender or decides after considering the written or oral evidence of the responsible medical officer to deal with the offender in some other way.

(6) The power of renewing an interim hospital order may be exercised without the offender being brought before the court if he is represented by counsel or a solicitor and his counsel or solicitor is given an opportunity of being heard.

(7) If an offender absconds from a hospital in which he is detained in pursuance of an interim hospital order, or while being conveyed to or from such a hospital, he may be arrested without warrant by a constable and shall, after being arrested, be brought as soon as practicable before the court that made the order ; and the court may thereupon terminate the order and deal with him in any way in which it could have dealt with him if no such order had been made.

## 39 Information as to hospitals

(1) Where a court is minded to make a hospital order or interim hospital order in respect of any person it may request—

- (a) the Regional Health Authority for the region in which that person resides or last resided; or
- (b) any other Regional Health Authority that appears to the court to be appropriate,

to furnish the court with such information as that Authority has or can reasonably obtain with respect to the hospital or hospitals (if any) in its region or elsewhere at which arrangements could be made for the admission of that person in pursuance of the order, and that Authority shall comply with any such request.

(2) In its application to Wales subsection (1) above shall have effect as if for any reference to any such Authority as is mentioned in paragraph (a) or (b) of that subsection there were substituted a reference to the Secretary of State, and as if for the words " in its region or elsewhere " there were substituted the words " in Wales " .

## 40 Effect of hospital orders, guardianship orders and interim hospital orders

(1) A hospital order shall be sufficient authority—

- (a) for a constable, an approved social worker or any other person directed to do so by the court to convey the patient to the hospital specified in the order within a period of 28 days ; and
- (b) for the managers of the hospital to admit him at any time within that period and thereafter detain him in accordance with the provisions of this Act.

(2) A guardianship order shall confer on the authority or person named in the order as guardian the same powers as a guardianship application made and accepted under Part II of this Act.

(3) Where an interim hospital order is made in respect of an offender—

- (a) a constable or any other person directed to do so by the court shall convey the offender to the hospital specified in the order within the period mentioned in section 38(4) above; and
- (b) the managers of the hospital shall admit him within that period and thereafter detain him in accordance with the provisions of section 38 above.

(4) A patient who is admitted to a hospital in pursuance of a hospital order, or placed under guardianship by a guardianship order, shall, subject to the provisions of this subsection, be treated for the purposes of the provisions of this Act mentioned in Part I of Schedule 1 to this Act as if he had been so admitted or placed on the date of the order in pursuance of an application for admission for treatment or a guardianship application, as the case may be, duly made under Part II of this Act, but subject to any modifications of those provisions specified in that Part of that Schedule.

(5) Where a patient is admitted to a hospital in pursuance of a hospital order, or placed under guardianship by a guardianship order, any previous application, hospital order or guardianship order by virtue of which he was liable to be detained in a hospital or subject to guardianship shall cease to have effect; but if the first-mentioned order, or the conviction on which it was made, is quashed on appeal, this subsection shall not apply and section 22 above shall have effect as if during any period for which the patient was liable to be detained or subject to guardianship under the order, he had been detained in custody as mentioned in that section.

*Restriction orders*

## 41 Power of higher courts to restrict discharge from hospital

(1) Where a hospital order is made in respect of an offender by the Crown Court, and it appears to the court, having regard to the nature of the offence, the antecedents of the offender and the risk of his committing further offences if set at large, that it is necessary for the protection of the public from serious harm so to do, the court may, subject to the provisions of this section, further order that the offender shall be subject to the special restrictions set out in this section, either without limit of time or during such period as may be specified in the order; and an order under this section shall be known as " a restriction order ".

(2) A restriction order shall not be made in the case of any person unless at least one of the registered medical practitioners whose evidence is taken into account by the court under section 37(2)(a) above has given evidence orally before the court.

(3) The special restrictions applicable to a patient in respect of whom a restriction order is in force are as follows—

- (a) none of the provisions of Part II of this Act relating to the duration, renewal and expiration of authority for the detention of patients shall apply, and the patient shall continue to be liable to be detained by virtue of the relevant hospital order until he is duly discharged under the said Part II or absolutely discharged under section 42, 73, 74 or 75 below ;
- (b) no application shall be made to a Mental Health Review Tribunal in respect of a patient under section 66 or 69(1) below;
- (c) the following powers shall be exercisable only with the consent of the Secretary of State, namely—
  - (i) power to grant leave of absence to the patient under section 17 above;
  - (ii) power to transfer the patient in pursuance of regulations under section 19 above ; and
  - (iii) power to order the discharge of the patient under section 23 above ;

and if leave of absence is granted under the said section 17 power to recall the patient under that section shall vest in the Secretary of State as well as the responsible medical officer; and

(d) the power of the Secretary of State to recall the patient under the said section 17 and power to take the patient into custody and return him under section 18 above may be exercised at any time;

and in relation to any such patient section 40(4) above shall have effect as if it referred to Part II of Schedule 1 to this Act instead of Part I of that Schedule.

(4) A hospital order shall not cease to have effect under section 40(5) above if a restriction order in respect of the patient is in force at the material time.

(5) Where a restriction order in respect of a patient ceases to have effect while the relevant hospital order continues in force, the provisions of section 40 above and Part I of Schedule 1 to this Act shall apply to the patient as if he had been admitted to the hospital in pursuance of a hospital order (without a restriction order) made on the date on which the restriction order ceased to have effect.

(6) While a person is subject to a restriction order the responsible medical officer shall at such intervals (not exceeding one year) as the Secretary of State may direct examine and report to the Secretary of State on that person ; and every report shall contain such particulars as the Secretary of State may require.

### 42 Powers of Secretary of State in respect of patients subject to restriction orders

(1) If the Secretary of State is satisfied that in the case of any patient a restriction order is no longer required for the protection of the public from serious harm, he may direct that the patient shall cease to be subject to the special restrictions set out in section 41(3) above ; and where the Secretary of State so directs, the restriction order shall cease to have effect, and section 41(5) above shall apply accordingly.

(2) At any time while a restriction order is in force in respect of a patient, the Secretary of State may, if he thinks fit, by warrant discharge the patient from hospital, either absolutely or subject to conditions; and where a person is absolutely discharged under this subsection, he shall thereupon cease to be liable to be detained by virtue of the relevant hospital order, and the restriction order shall cease to have effect accordingly.

(3) The Secretary of State may at any time during the continuance in force of a restriction order in respect of a patient who has been conditionally discharged under subsection (2) above by warrant recall the patient to such hospital as may be specified in the warrant.

(4) Where a patient is recalled as mentioned in subsection (3) above—

(a) if the hospital specified in the warrant is not the hospital from which the patient was conditionally discharged, the hospital order and the restriction order shall have effect as if the hospital specified in the warrant were substituted for the hospital specified in the hospital order;

(b) in any case, the patient shall be treated for the purposes of section 18 above as if he had absented himself without leave from the hospital specified in the warrant, and, if the restriction order was made for a specified period, that period shall not in any event expire until the patient returns to the hospital or is returned to the hospital under that section.

(5) If a restriction order in respect of a patient ceases to have effect after the patient has been conditionally discharged under this section, the patient shall, unless previously recalled under subsection (3) above, be deemed to be absolutely discharged on the date when the order ceases to have effect, and shall cease to be liable to be detained by virtue of the relevant hospital order accordingly.

(6) The Secretary of State may, if satisfied that the attendance at any place in Great Britain of a patient who is subject to a restriction order is desirable in the interests of justice or for the purposes of any public inquiry, direct him to be taken to that place; and where a patient is directed under this subsection to be taken to any place he shall, unless the Secretary of State otherwise directs, be kept in custody while being so taken, while at that place and while being taken back to the hospital in which he is liable to be detained.

### 43 Power of magistrates' courts to commit for restriction order

(1) If in the case of a person of or over the age of 14 years who is convicted by a magistrates' court of an offence punishable on summary conviction with imprisonment—
- (a) the conditions which under section 37(1) above are required to be satisfied for the making of a hospital order are satisfied in respect of the offender; but
- (b) it appears to the court, having regard to the nature of the offence, the antecedents of the offender and the risk of his committing further offences if set at large, that if a hospital order is made a restriction order should also be made,

the court may, instead of making a hospital order or dealing with him in any other manner, commit him in custody to the Crown Court to be dealt with in respect of the offence.

(2) Where an offender is committed to the Crown Court under this section, the Crown Court shall inquire into the circumstances of the case and may—
- (a) if that court would have power so to do under the foregoing provisions of this Part of this Act upon the conviction of the offender before that court of such an offence as is described in section 37(1) above, make a hospital order in his case, with or without a restriction order;
- (b) if the court does not make such an order, deal with the offender in any other manner in which the magistrates' court might have dealt with him.

(3) The Crown Court shall have the same power to make orders under sections 35, 36 and 38 above in the case of a person committed to the court under this section as the Crown Court has under those sections in the case of an accused person within the meaning of section 35 or 36 above or of a person convicted before that court as mentioned in section 38 above.

(4) The power of a magistrates' court under section 38 of the Magistrates' Courts Act 1980 (which enables such a court to commit an offender to the Crown Court where the court is of the opinion that greater punishment should be inflicted for the offence than the court has power to inflict) shall also be exercisable by a magistrates' court where it is of the opinion that greater punishment should be inflicted as aforesaid on the offender unless a hospital order is made in his case with a restriction order.

(5) The power of the Crown Court to make a hospital order, with or without a restriction order, in the case of a person convicted before that court of an offence may, in the

same circumstances and subject to the same conditions, be exercised by such a court in the case of a person committed to the court under section 5 of the Vagrancy Act 1824 (which provides for the committal to the Crown Court of persons who are incorrigible rogues within the meaning of that section).

## 44 Committal to hospital under s. 43

(1) Where an offender is committed under section 43(1) above and the magistrates' court by which he is committed is satisfied on written or oral evidence that arrangements have been made for the admission of the offender to a hospital in the event of an order being made under this section, the court may, instead of committing him in custody, by order direct him to be admitted to that hospital, specifying it, and to be detained there until the case is disposed of by the Crown Court, and may give such directions as it thinks fit for his production from the hospital to attend the Crown Court by which his case is to be dealt with.

(2) The evidence required by subsection (1) above shall be given by the registered medical practitioner who would be in charge of the offender's treatment or by some other person representing the managers of the hospital in question.

(3) The power to give directions under section 37(4) above, section 37(5) above and section 40(1) above shall apply in relation to an order under this section as they apply in relation to a hospital order, but as if references to the period of 28 days mentioned in section 40(1) above were omitted; and subject as aforesaid an order under this section shall, until the offender's case is disposed of by the Crown Court, have the same effect as a hospital order together with a restriction order, made without limitation of time.

## 45 Appeals from magistrates' courts

(1) Where on the trial of an information charging a person with an offence a magistrates' court makes a hospital order or guardianship order in respect of him without convicting him, he shall have the same right of appeal against the order as if it had been made on his conviction; and on any such appeal the Crown Court shall have the same powers as if the appeal had been against both conviction and sentence.

(2) An appeal by a child or young person with respect to whom any such order has been made, whether the appeal is against the order or against the finding upon which the order was made, may be brought by him or by his parent or guardian on his behalf.

*Detention during Her Majesty's pleasure*

## 46 Persons ordered to be kept in custody during Her Majesty's pleasure

(1) The Secretary of State may by warrant direct that any person who, by virtue of any enactment to which this subsection applies, is required to be kept in custody during Her Majesty's pleasure or until the directions of Her Majesty are known shall be detained in such hospital (not being a mental nursing home) as may be specified in the warrant and, where that person is not already detained in the hospital, give directions for his removal there.

(2) The enactments to which subsection (1) above applies are section 16 of the Courts-Martial (Appeals) Act 1968, section 116 of the Army Act 1955, section 116 of the Air Force Act 1955 and section 63 of the Naval Discipline Act 1957.

(3) A direction under this section in respect of any person shall have the same effect as a hospital order together with a restriction order, made without limitation of time; and where such a direction is given in respect of a person while he is in the hospital, he shall be deemed to be admitted in pursuance of, and on the date of, the direction.

*Transfer to hospital of prisoners, etc.*

### 47 Removal to hospital of persons serving sentences of imprisonment, etc.

(1) if in the case of a person serving a sentence of imprisonment the Secretary of State is satisfied, by reports from at least two registered medical practitioners—

- (a) that the said person is suffering from mental illness, psychopathic disorder, severe mental impairment or mental impairment; and
- (b) that the mental disorder from which that person is suffering is of a nature or degree which makes it appropriate for him to be detained in a hospital for medical treatment and, in the case of psychopathic disorder or mental impairment, that such treatment is likely to alleviate or prevent a deterioration of his condition ;

the Secretary of State may, if he is of the opinion having regard to the public interest and all the circumstances that it is expedient so to do, by warrant direct that that person be removed to and detained in such hospital (not being a mental nursing home) as may be specified in the direction; and a direction under this section shall be known as " a transfer direction ".

(2) A transfer direction shall cease to have effect at the expiration of the period of 14 days beginning with the date on which it is given unless within that period the person with respect to whom it was given has been received into the hospital specified in the direction.

(3) A transfer direction with respect to any person shall have the same effect as a hospital order made in his case.

(4) A transfer direction shall specify the form or forms of mental disorder referred to in paragraph (a) of subsection (1) above from which, upon the reports taken into account under that subsection, the patient is found by the Secretary of State to be suffering; and no such direction shall be given unless the patient is described in each of those reports as suffering from the same form of disorder, whether or not he is also described in either of them as suffering from another form.

(5) References in this Part of this Act to a person serving a sentence of imprisonment include references—

- (a) to a person detained in pursuance of any sentence or order for detention made by a court in criminal proceedings (other than an order under any enactment to which section 46 above applies);
- (b) to a person committed to custody under section 115(3) of the Magistrates' Courts Act 1980 (which relates to persons who fail to comply with an order to enter into recognisances to keep the peace or be of good behaviour) ; and
- (c) to a person committed by a court to a prison or other institution to which the Prison Act 1952 applies in default of payment of any sum adjudged to be paid on his conviction.

### 48 Removal to hospital of other prisoners

(1) If in the case of a person to whom this section applies the Secretary of State is satisfied by the same reports as are required for the purposes of section 47 above that that person is suffering from mental illness or severe mental impairment of a nature or degree which makes it appropriate for him to be detained in a hospital for medical treatment and that he is in urgent need of such treatment, the Secretary of State shall have the same power of giving a transfer direction in respect of him under that section as if he were serving a sentence of imprisonment.

(2) This section applies to the following persons, that is to say—

- (a) persons detained in a prison or remand centre, not being persons serving a sentence of imprisonment or persons falling within the following paragraphs of this subsection;
- (b) persons remanded in custody by a magistrates' court;
- (c) civil prisoners, that is to say, persons committed by a court to prison for a limited term (including persons committed to prison in pursuance of a writ of attachment), who are not persons falling to be dealt with under section 47 above ;
- (d) persons detained under the Immigration Act 1971.

(3) Subsections (2) to (4) of section 47 above shall apply for the purposes of this section and of any transfer direction given by virtue of this section as they apply for the purposes of that section and of any transfer direction under that section.

### 49 Restriction on discharge of prisoners removed to hospital

(1) Where a transfer direction is given in respect of any person, the Secretary of State, if he thinks fit, may by warrant further direct that that person shall be subject to the special restrictions set out in section 41 above; and where the Secretary of State gives a transfer direction in respect of any such person as is described in paragraph (a) or (b) of section 48(2) above, he shall also give a direction under this section applying those restrictions to him.

(2) A direction under this section shall have the same effect as a restriction order made under section 41 above and shall be known as " a restriction direction ".

(3) While a person is subject to a restriction direction the responsible medical officer shall at such intervals (not exceeding one year) as the Secretary of State may direct examine and report to the Secretary of State on that person; and every report shall contain such particulars as the Secretary of State may require.

### 50 Further provisions as to prisoners under sentence

(1) Where a transfer direction and a restriction direction have been given in respect of a person serving a sentence of imprisonment and before the expiration of that person's sentence the Secretary of State is notified by the responsible medical officer, any other registered medical practitioner or a Mental Health Review Tribunal that that person no longer requires treatment in hospital for mental disorder or that no effective treatment for his disorder can be given in the hospital to which he has been removed, the Secretary of State may—

(a) by warrant direct that he be remitted to any prison or other institution in which he might have been detained if he had not been removed to hospital, there to be dealt with as if he had not been so removed; or

(b) exercise any power of releasing him on licence or discharging him under supervision which would have been exercisable if he had been remitted to such a prison or institution as aforesaid,

and on his arrival in the prison or other institution or, as the case may be, his release or discharge as aforesaid, the transfer direction and the restriction direction shall cease to have effect.

(2) A restriction direction in the case of a person serving a sentence of imprisonment shall cease to have effect on the expiration of the sentence.

(3) Subject to subsection (4) below, references in this section to the expiration of a person's sentence are references to the expiration of the period during which he would have been liable to be detained in a prison or other institution if the transfer direction had not been given and that period shall be treated as expiring on the date on which he could have been discharged if he had not forfeited remission of any part of the sentence after his removal pursuant to the direction.

(4) For the purposes of section 49(2) of the Prison Act 1952 (which provides for discounting from the sentences of certain prisoners periods while they are unlawfully at large) a patient who, having been transferred in pursuance of a transfer direction from any such institution as is referred to in that section, is at large in circumstances in which he is liable to be taken into custody under any provision of this Act, shall be treated as unlawfully at large and absent from that institution.

### 51 Further provisions as to detained persons

(1) This section has effect where a transfer direction has been given in respect of any such person as is described in paragraph (a) of section 48(2) above and that person is in this section referred to as " the detainee ".

(2) The transfer direction shall cease to have effect when the detainee's case is disposed of by the court having jurisdiction to try or otherwise deal with him, but without prejudice to any power of that court to make a hospital order or other order under this Part of this Act in his case.

(3) If the Secretary of State is notified by the responsible medical officer, any other registered medical practitioner or a Mental Health Review Tribunal at any time before the detainee's case is disposed of by that court—

(a) that the detainee no longer requires treatment in hospital for mental disorder; or

(b) that no effective treatment for his disorder can be given at the hospital to which he has been removed,

the Secretary of State may by warrant direct that he be remitted to any place where he might have been detained if he had not been removed to hospital, there to be dealt with as if he had not been so removed, and on his arrival at the place to which he is so remitted the transfer direction shall cease to have effect.

(4) If (no direction having been given under subsection (3) above) the court having jurisdiction to try or otherwise deal with the detainee is satisfied on the written or oral evidence of the responsible medical officer—

(a) that the detainee no longer requires treatment in hospital for mental disorder; or

(b) that no effective treatment for his disorder can be given at the hospital to which he has been removed,

the court may order him to be remitted to any such place as is mentioned in subsection (3) above or released on bail and on his arrival at that place or, as the case may be, his release on bail the transfer direction shall cease to have effect.

(5) If (no direction or order having been given or made under subsection (3) or (4) above) it appears to the court having jurisdiction to try or otherwise deal with the detainee—

(a) that it is impracticable or inappropriate to bring the detainee before the court; and

(b) that the conditions set out in subsection (6) below are satisfied,

the court may make a hospital order (with or without a restriction order) in his case in his absence and, in the case of a person awaiting trial, without convicting him.

(6) A hospital order may be made in respect of a person under subsection (5) above if the court—

(a) is satisfied, on the written or oral evidence of at least two registered medical practitioners, that the detainee is suffering from mental illness or severe mental impairment of a nature or degree which makes it appropriate for the patient to be detained in a hospital for medical treatment; and

(b) is of the opinion, after considering any depositions or other documents required to be sent to the proper officer of the court, that it is proper to make such an order.

(7) Where a person committed to the Crown Court to be dealt with under section 43 above is admitted to a hospital in pursuance of an order under section 44 above, subsections (5) and (6) above shall apply as if he were a person subject to a transfer direction.

### 52 Further provisions as to persons remanded by magistrates' courts

(1) This section has effect where a transfer direction has been given in respect of any such person as is described in paragraph (b) of section 48(2) above ; and that person is in this section referred to as " the accused ".

(2) Subject to subsection (5) below, the transfer direction shall cease to have effect on the expiration of the period of remand unless the accused is committed in custody to the Crown Court for trial or to be otherwise dealt with.

(3) Subject to subsection (4) below, the power of further remanding the accused under section 128 of the Magistrates' Courts Act 1980 may be exercised by the court without his being brought before the court; and if the court further remands the accused in custody (whether or not he is brought before the court) the period of remand shall, for the purposes of this section, be deemed not to have expired.

(4) The court shall not under subsection (3) above further remand the accused in his absence unless he has appeared before the court within the previous six months.

(5) If the magistrates' court is satisfied, on the written or oral evidence of the responsible medical officer—

(a) that the accused no longer requires treatment in hospital for mental disorder; or

(b) that no effective treatment for his disorder can be given in the hospital to which he has been removed,

the court may direct that the transfer direction shall cease to have effect notwithstanding that the period of remand has not expired or that the accused is committed to the Crown Court as mentioned in subsection (2) above.

(6) If the accused is committed to the Crown Court as mentioned in subsection (2) above and the transfer direction has not ceased to have effect under subsection (5) above, section 51 above shall apply as if the transfer direction given in his case were a direction given in respect of a person falling within that section.

(7) The magistrates' court may, in the absence of the accused, inquire as examining justices into an offence alleged to have been committed by him and commit him for trial in accordance with section 6 of the Magistrates' Courts Act 1980 if—

(a) the court is satisfied, on the written or oral evidence of the responsible medical officer, that the accused is unfit to take part in the proceedings; and

(b) where the court proceeds under subsection (1) of that section, the accused is represented by counsel or a solicitor.

## 53 Further provisions as to civil prisoners and persons detained under the Immigration Act 1971

(1) Subject to subsection (2) below, a transfer direction given in respect of any such person as is described in paragraph (c) or (d) of section 48(2) above shall cease to have effect on the expiration of the period during which he would, but for his removal to hospital, be liable to be detained in the place from which he was removed.

(2) Where a transfer direction and a restriction direction have been given in respect of any such person as is mentioned in subsection (1) above, then, if the Secretary of State is notified by the responsible medical officer, any other registered medical practitioner or a Mental Health Review Tribunal at any time before the expiration of the period there mentioned—

(a) that that person no longer requires treatment in hospital for mental disorder; or

(b) that no effective treatment for his disorder can be given in the hospital to which he has been removed,

the Secretary of State may by warrant direct that he be remitted to any place where he might have been detained if he had not been removed to hospital, and on his arrival at the place to which he is so remitted the transfer direction and the restriction direction shall cease to have effect.

### *Supplemental*

## 54 Requirements as to medical evidence

(1) The registered medical practitioner whose evidence is taken into account under section 35(3)(a) above and at least one of the registered medical practitioners whose evidence is taken into account under sections 36(1), 37(2)(a), 38(1) and 51(6)(a) above and whose reports are taken into account under sections 47(1) and 48(1) above shall be a practitioner approved for the purposes of section 12 above by the Secretary of State as having special experience in the diagnosis or treatment of mental disorder.

(2) For the purposes of any provision of this Part of this Act under which a court may act on the written evidence of—

(a) a registered medical practitioner or a registered medical practitioner of any description; or

(b) a person representing the managers of a hospital,

a report in writing purporting to be signed by a registered medical practitioner or a registered medical practitioner of such a description or by a person representing the managers of a hospital may, subject to the provisions of this section, be received in evidence without proof of the signature of the practitioner or that person and without proof that he has the requisite qualifications or authority or is of the requisite description; but the court may require the signatory of any such report to be called to give oral evidence.

(3) Where, in pursuance of a direction of the court, any such report is tendered in evidence otherwise than by or on behalf of the person who is the subject of the report, then—

(a) if that person is represented by counsel or a solicitor, a copy of the report shall be given to his counsel or solicitor;

(b) if that person is not so represented, the substance of the report shall be disclosed to him or, where he is a child or young person, to his parent or guardian if present in court; and

(c) except where the report relates only to arrangements for his admission to a hospital, that person may require the signatory of the report to be called to give oral evidence, and evidence to rebut the evidence contained in the report may be called by or on behalf of that person.

## 55 Interpretation of Part III

(1) In this Part of this Act—

" child " and " young person " have the same meaning as in the Children and Young Persons Act 1933 ;

"civil prisoner" has the meaning given to it by section 48(2)(c) above;

"guardian", in relation to a child or young person, has the same meaning as in the Children and Young Persons Act 1933 ;

" place of safety ", in relation to a person who is not a child or young person, means any police station, prison or remand centre, or any hospital the managers of which are willing temporarily to receive him, and in relation to a child or young person has the same meaning as in the Children and Young Persons Act 1933 ;

"responsible medical officer", in relation to a person liable to be detained in a hospital within the meaning of Part II of this Act, means the registered medical practitioner in charge of the treatment of the patient.

(2) Any reference in this Part of this Act to an offence punishable on summary conviction with imprisonment shall be construed without regard to any prohibition or restriction imposed by or under any enactment relating to the imprisonment of young offenders.

(3) Where a patient who is liable to be detained in a hospital in pursuance of an order or direction under this Part of this Act is treated by virtue of any provision of this Part of this Act as if he had been admitted to the hospital in pursuance of a subsequent order or direction under this Part of this Act or a subsequent application for admission for treatment under Part II of this Act, he shall be treated as if the subsequent order,

direction or application had described him as suffering from the form or forms of mental disorder specified in the earlier order or direction or, where he is treated as if he had been so admitted by virtue of a direction under section 42(1) above, such form of mental disorder as may be specified in the direction under that section.

(4) Any reference to a hospital order, a guardianship order or a restriction order in section 40(2), (4) or (5), section 41(3) to (5), or section 42 above or section 69(1) below shall be construed as including a reference to any order or direction under this Part of this Act having the same effect as the first-mentioned order; and the exceptions and modifications set out in Schedule 1 to this Act in respect of the provisions of this Act described in that Schedule accordingly include those which are consequential on the provisions of this subsection.

(5) Section 34(2) above shall apply for the purposes of this Part of this Act as it applies for the purposes of Part II of this Act.

(6) References in this Part of this Act to persons serving a sentence of imprisonment shall be construed in accordance with section 47(5) above.

(7) Section 99 of the Children and Young Persons Act 1933 (which relates to the presumption and determination of age) shall apply for the purposes of this Part of this Act as it applies for the purposes of that Act.

## PART IV

### Consent to Treatment

### 56 Patients to whom Part IV applies

(1) This Part of this Act applies to any patient liable to be detained under this Act except—

- (a) a patient who is liable to be detained by virtue of an emergency application and in respect of whom the second medical recommendation referred to in section 4(4)(a) above has not been given and received ;
- (b) a patient who is liable to be detained by virtue of section 5(2) or (4) or 35 above or section 135 or 136 below or by virtue of a direction under section 37(4) above; and
- (c) a patient who has been conditionally discharged under section 42(2) above or section 73 or 74 below and has not been recalled to hospital.

(2) Section 57 and, so far as relevant to that section, sections 59, 60 and 62 below, apply also to any patient who is not liable to be detained under this Act.

### 57 Treatment requiring consent and a second opinion

(1) This section applies to the following forms of medical treatment for mental disorder—

- (a) any surgical operation for destroying brain tissue or for destroying the functioning of brain tissue ; and
- (b) such other forms of treatment as may be specified for the purposes of this section by regulations made by the Secretary of State.

(2) Subject to section 62 below, a patient shall not be given any form of treatment to which this section applies unless he has consented to it and—

(a) a registered medical practitioner appointed for the purposes of this Part of this Act by the Secretary of State (not being the responsible medical officer) and two other persons appointed for the purposes of this paragraph by the Secretary of State (not being registered medical practitioners) have certified in writing that the patient is capable of understanding the nature, purpose and likely effects of the treatment in question and has consented to it; and (b) the registered medical practitioner referred to in paragraph (a) above has certified in writing that, having regard to the likelihood of the treatment alleviating or preventing a deterioration of the patient's condition, the treatment should be given.

(3) Before giving a certificate under subsection (2)(b) above the registered medical practitioner concerned shall consult two other persons who have been professionally concerned with the patient's medical treatment, and of those persons one shall be a nurse and the other shall be neither a nurse nor a registered medical practitioner.

(4) Before making any regulations for the purpose of this section the Secretary of State shall consult such bodies as appear to him to be concerned.

## 58 Treatment requiring consent or a second opinion

(1) This section applies to the following forms of medical treatment for mental disorder—

(a) such forms of treatment as may be specified for the purposes of this section by regulations made by the Secretary of State;

(b) the administration of medicine to a patient by any means (not being a form of treatment specified under paragraph (a) above or section 57 above) at any time during a period for which he is liable to be detained as a patient to whom this Part of this Act applies if three months or more have elapsed since the first occasion in that period when medicine was administered to him by any means for his mental disorder.

(2) The Secretary of State may by order vary the length of the period mentioned in subsection (1)(b) above.

(3) Subject to section 62 below, a patient shall not be given any form of treatment to which this section applies unless—

(a) he has consented to that treatment and either the responsible medical officer or a registered medical practitioner appointed for the purposes of this Part of this Act by the Secretary of State has certified in writing that the patient is capable of understanding its nature, purpose and likely effects and has consented to it; or

(b) a registered medical practitioner appointed as aforesaid (not being the responsible medical officer) has certified in writing that the patient is not capable of understanding the nature, purpose and likely effects of that treatment or has not consented to it but that, having regard to the likelihood of its alleviating or preventing a deterioration of his condition, the treatment should be given.

(4) Before giving a certificate under subsection (3)(b) above the registered medical practitioner concerned shall consult two other persons who have been professionally concerned with the patient's medical treatment, and of those persons one shall be a nurse and the other shall be neither a nurse nor a registered medical practitioner.

(5) Before making any regulations for the purposes of this section the Secretary of State shall consult such bodies as appear to him to be concerned.

### 59 Plans of treatment

Any consent or certificate under section 57 or 58 above may relate to a plan of treatment under which the patient is to be given (whether within a specified period or otherwise) one or more of the forms of treatment to which that section applies.

### 60 Withdrawal of consent

(1) Where the consent of a patient to any treatment has been given for the purposes of section 57 or 58 above, the patient may, subject to section 62 below, at any time before the completion of the treatment withdraw his consent, and those sections shall then apply as if the remainder of the treatment were a separate form of treatment.

(2) Without prejudice to the application of subsection (1) above to any treatment given under the plan of treatment to which a patient has consented, a patient who has consented to such a plan may, subject to section 62 below, at any time withdraw his consent to further treatment, or to further treatment of any description, under the plan.

### 61 Review of treatment

(1) Where a patient is given treatment in accordance with section 57(2) or 58(3)(b) above a report on the treatment and the patient's condition shall be given by the responsible medical officer to the Secretary of State—

- (a) on the next occasion on which the responsible medical officer furnishes a report in respect of the patient under section 20(3) above ; and
- (b) at any other time if so required by the Secretary of State.

(2) In relation to a patient who is subject to a restriction order or restriction direction subsection (1) above shall have effect as if paragraph (a) required the report to be made—

- (a) in the case of treatment in the period of six months beginning with the date of the order or direction, at the end of that period ;
- (b) in the case of treatment at any subsequent time, on the next occasion on which the responsible medical officer makes a report in respect of the patient under section 41(6) or 49(3) above.

(3) The Secretary of State may at any time give notice to the responsible medical officer directing that, subject to section 62 below, a certificate given in respect of a patient under section 57(2) or 58(3)(b) above shall not apply to treatment given to him after a date specified in the notice and sections 57 and 58 above shall then apply to any such treatment as if that certificate had not been given.

### 62 Urgent treatment

(1) Sections 57 and 58 above shall not apply to any treatment—

- (a) which is immediately necessary to save the patient's life ; or
- (b) which (not being irreversible) is immediately necessary to prevent a serious deterioration of his condition ; or

(c) which (not being irreversible or hazardous) is immediately necessary to alleviate serious suffering by the patient; or

(d) which (not being irreversible or hazardous) is immediately necessary and represents the minimum interference necessary to prevent the patient from behaving violently or being a danger to himself or to others.

(2) Sections 60 and 61(3) above shall not preclude the continuation of any treatment or of treatment under any plan pending compliance with section 57 or 58 above if the responsible medical officer considers that the discontinuance of the treatment or of treatment under the plan would cause serious suffering to the patient.

(3) For the purposes of this section treatment is irreversible if it has unfavourable irreversible physical or psychological consequences and hazardous if it entails significant physical hazard.

### 63 Treatment not requiring consent

The consent of a patient shall not be required for any medical treatment given to him for the mental disorder from which he is suffering, not being treatment falling within section 57 or 58 above, if the treatment is given by or under the direction of the responsible medical officer.

### 64 Supplementary provisions for Part IV

(1) In this Part of this Act "the responsible medical officer " means the registered medical practitioner in charge of the treatment of the patient in question and " hospital " includes a mental nursing home.

(2) Any certificate for the purposes of this Part of this Act shall be in such form as may be prescribed by regulations made by the Secretary of State.

## PART V

MENTAL HEALTH REVIEW TRIBUNALS

*Constitution etc.*

### 65 Mental Health Review Tribunals

(1) There shall continue to be a tribunal known as a Mental Health Review Tribunal for every region for which a Regional Health Authority is established in pursuance of the National Health Service Act 1977 and for Wales, for the purpose of dealing with applications and references by and in respect of patients under the provisions of this Act.

(2) The provisions of Schedule 2 to this Act shall have effect with respect to the constitution of Mental Health Review Tribunals.

(3) Subject to the provisions of Schedule 2 to this Act, and to rules made by the Lord Chancellor under this Act, the jurisdiction of a Mental Health Review Tribunal may be exercised by any three or more of its members, and references in this Act to a Mental Health Review Tribunal shall be construed accordingly.

(4) The Secretary of State may pay to the members of Mental Health Review Tribunals such remuneration and allowances as he may with the consent of the Treasury determine, and defray the expenses of such tribunals to such amount as he may with the consent of the Treasury determine, and may provide for each such tribunal such officers and servants, and such accommodation, as the tribunal may require.

*Applications and references concerning Part II patients*

### 66 Applications to tribunals

(1) Where—

(a) a patient is admitted to a hospital in pursuance of an application for admission for assessment; or

(b) a patient is admitted to a hospital in pursuance of an application for admission for treatment; or

(c) a patient is received into guardianship in pursuance of a guardianship application; or

(d) a report is furnished under section 16 above in respect of a patient; or

(e) a patient is transferred from guardianship to a hospital in pursuance of regulations made under section 19 above; or

(f) a report is furnished under section 20 above in respect of a patient and the patient is not discharged ; or

(g) a report is furnished under section 25 above in respect of a patient who is detained in pursuance of an application for admission for treatment; or

(h) an order is made under section 29 above in respect of a patient who is or subsequently becomes liable to be detained or subject to guardianship under Part II of this Act,

an application may be made to a Mental Health Review Tribunal within the relevant period—

(i) by the patient (except in the cases mentioned in paragraphs (g) and (h) above) or, in the case mentioned in paragraph (d) above, by his nearest relative, and

(ii) in the cases mentioned in paragraphs (g) and (h) above, by his nearest relative.

(2) In subsection (1) above " the relevant period " means—

(a) in the case mentioned in paragraph (a) of that subsection, 14 days beginning with the day on which the patient is admitted as so mentioned ;

(b) in the case mentioned in paragraph (b) of that subsection, six months beginning with the day on which the patient is admitted as so mentioned ;

(c) in the case mentioned in paragraph (c) of that subsection, six months beginning with the day on which the application is accepted;

(d) in the cases mentioned in paragraphs (d) and (g) of that subsection, 28 days beginning with the day on which the applicant is informed that the report has been furnished;

(e) in the case mentioned in paragraph (e) of that subsection, six months beginning with the day on which the patient is transferred;

(f) in the case mentioned in paragraph (f) of that subsection, the period for which authority for the patient's detention or guardianship is renewed by virtue of the report;

(g) in the case mentioned in paragraph (h) of that subsection, 12 months beginning with the date of the order, and in any subsequent period of 12 months during which the order continues in force.

(3) Section 32 above shall apply for the purposes of this section as it applies for the purposes of Part II of this Act.

## 67 References to tribunals by Secretary of State concerning Part II patients

(1) The Secretary of State may, if he thinks fit, at any time refer to a Mental Health Review Tribunal the case of any patient who is liable to be detained or subject to guardianship under Part II of this Act.

(2) For the purpose of furnishing information for the purposes of a reference under subsection (1) above any registered medical practitioner authorised by or on behalf of the patient may, at any reasonable time, visit the patient and examine him in private and require the production of and inspect any records relating to the detention or treatment of the patient in any hospital.

(3) Section 32 above shall apply for the purposes of this section as it applies for the purposes of Part II of this Act.

## 68 Duty of managers of hospitals to refer cases to tribunal

(1) Where a patient who is admitted to a hospital in pursuance of an application for admission for treatment or a patient who is transferred from guardianship to hospital does not exercise his right to apply to a Mental Health Review Tribunal under section 66(1) above by virtue of his case falling within paragraph (b) or, as the case may be, paragraph (e) of that section, the managers of the hospital shall at the expiration of the period for making such an application refer the patient's case to such a tribunal unless an application or reference in respect of the patient has then been made under section 66(1) above by virtue of his case falling within paragraph (d), (g) or (h) of that section or under section 67(1) above.

(2) If the authority for the detention of a patient in a hospital is renewed under section 20 above and a period of three years (or, if the patient has not attained the age of sixteen years, one year) has elapsed since his case was last considered by a Mental Health Review Tribunal, whether on his own application or otherwise, the managers of the hospital shall refer his case to such a tribunal.

(3) For the purpose of furnishing information for the purposes of any reference under this section, any registered medical practitioner authorised by or on behalf of the patient may at any reasonable time visit and examine the patient in private and require the production of and inspect any records relating to the detention or treatment of the patient in any hospital.

(4) The Secretary of State may by order vary the length of the periods mentioned in subsection (2) above.

(5) For the purposes of subsection (1) above a person who applies to a tribunal but subsequently withdraws his application shall be treated as not having exercised his right to apply, and where a person withdraws his application on a date after the expiration of the period mentioned in that subsection, the managers shall refer the patient's case as soon as possible after that date.

*Applications and references concerning Part III patients*

**69 Applications to tribunals concerning patients subject to hospital and guardianship orders**

(1) Without prejudice to any provision of section 66(1) above as applied by section 40(4) above, an application to a Mental Health Review Tribunal may also be made—

(a) in respect of a patient admitted to a hospital in pursuance of a hospital order, by the nearest relative of the patient in the period between the expiration of six months and the expiration of 12 months beginning with the date of the order and in any subsequent period of 12 months; and

(b) in respect of a patient placed under guardianship by a guardianship order—

(i) by the patient, within the period of six months beginning with the date of the order;

(ii) by the nearest relative of the patient, within the period of 12 months beginning with the date of the order and in any subsequent period of 12 months.

(2) Where a person detained in a hospital—

(a) is treated as subject to a hospital order or transfer direction by virtue of section 41(5) above, 82(2) or 85(2) below, section 73(2) of the Mental Health (Scotland) Act 1960 or section 5(1) of the Criminal Procedure (Insanity) Act 1964 ; or

(b) is subject to a direction having the same effect as a hospital order by virtue of section 46(3), 47(3) or 48(3) above,

then, without prejudice to any provision of Part II of this Act as applied by section 40 above, that person may make an application to a Mental Health Review Tribunal in the period of six months beginning with the date of the order or direction mentioned in paragraph (a) above or, as the case may be, the date of the direction mentioned in paragraph (b) above.

**70 Applications to tribunals concerning restricted patients**

A patient who is a restricted patient within the meaning of section 79 below and is detained in a hospital may apply to a Mental Health Review Tribunal—

(a) in the period between the expiration of six months and the expiration of 12 months beginning with the date of the relevant hospital order or transfer direction; and

(b) in any subsequent period of 12 months.

**71 References by Secretary of State concerning restricted patients**

(1) The Secretary of State may at any time refer the case of a restricted patient to a Mental Health Review Tribunal.

(2) The Secretary of State shall refer to a Mental Health Review Tribunal the case of any restricted patient detained in a hospital whose case has not been considered by such a tribunal, whether on his own application or otherwise, within the last three years.

(3) The Secretary of State may by order vary the length of the period mentioned in subsection (2) above.

(4) Any reference under subsection (1) above in respect of a patient who has been conditionally discharged and not recalled to hospital shall be made to the tribunal for the area in which the patient resides.

(5) Where a person who is treated as subject to a hospital order and a restriction order by virtue of an order under section 5(1) of the Criminal Procedure (Insanity) Act 1964 does not exercise his right to apply to a Mental Health Review Tribunal in the period of six months beginning with the date of that order, the Secretary of State shall at the expiration of that period refer his case to a tribunal.

(6) For the purposes of subsection (5) above a person who applies to a tribunal but subsequently withdraws his application shall be treated as not having exercised his right to apply, and where a patient withdraws his application on a date after the expiration of the period there mentioned the Secretary of State shall refer his case as soon as possible after that date.

*Discharge of patients*

### 72 Powers of tribunals

(1) Where application is made to a Mental Health Review Tribunal by or in respect of a patient who is liable to be detained under this Act, the tribunal may in any case direct that the patient be discharged, and—

- (a) the tribunal shall direct the discharge of a patient liable to be detained under section 2 above if they are satisfied—
  - (i) that he is not then suffering from mental disorder or from mental disorder of a nature or degree which warrants his detention in a hospital for assessment (or for assessment followed by medical treatment) for at least a limited period ; or
  - (ii) that his detention as aforesaid is not justified in the interests of his own health or safety or with a view to the protection of other persons ;
- (b) the tribunal shall direct the discharge of a patient liable to be detained otherwise than under section 2 above if they are satisfied—
  - (i) that he is not then suffering from mental illness, psychopathic disorder, severe mental impairment or mental impairment or from any of those forms of disorder of a nature or degree which makes it appropriate for him to be liable to be detained in a hospital; for medical treatment; or
  - (ii) that it is not necessary for the health or safety of the patient or for the protection of other persons that he should receive such treatment; or
  - (iii) in the case of an application by virtue of paragraph (g) of section 66(1) above, that the patient, if released, would not be likely to act in a manner dangerous to other persons or to himself.

(2) In determining whether to direct the discharge of a patient detained otherwise than under section 2 above in a case not falling within paragraph (b) of subsection (1) above, the tribunal shall have regard—

- (a) to the likelihood of medical treatment alleviating or preventing a deterioration of the patient's condition; and
- (b) in the case of a patient suffering from mental illness or severe mental impairment, to the likelihood of the patient, if discharged, being able to care

for himself, to obtain the care he needs or to guard himself against serious exploitation.

(3) A tribunal may under subsection (1) above direct the discharge of a patient on a future date specified in the direction; and where a tribunal do not direct the discharge of a patient under that subsection the tribunal may—

(a) with a view to facilitating his discharge on a future date, recommend that he be granted leave of absence or transferred to another hospital or into guardianship; and

(b) further consider his case in the event of any such recommendation not being complied with.

(4) Where application is made to a Mental Health Review Tribunal by or in respect of a patient who is subject to guardianship under this Act, the tribunal may in any case direct that the patient be discharged, and shall so direct if they are satisfied—

(a) that he is not then suffering from mental illness, psychopathic disorder, severe mental impairment or mental impairment; or

(b) that it is not necessary in the interests of the welfare of the patient, or for the protection of other persons, that the patient should remain under such guardianship.

(5) Where application is made to a Mental Health Review Tribunal under any provision of this Act by or in respect of a patient and the tribunal do not direct that the patient be discharged, the tribunal may, if satisfied that the patient is suffering from a form of mental disorder other than the form specified in the application, order or direction relating to him, direct that that application, order or direction be amended by substituting for the form of mental disorder specified in it such other form of mental disorder as appears to the tribunal to be appropriate.

(6) Subsections (1) to (5) above apply in relation to references to a Mental Health Review Tribunal as they apply in relation to applications made to such a tribunal by or in respect of a patient

(7) Subsection (1) above shall not apply in the case of a restricted patient except as provided in sections 73 and 74 below.

### 73 Power to discharge restricted patients

(1) Where an application to a Mental Health Review Tribunal is made by a restricted patient who is subject to a restriction order, or where the case of such a patient is referred to such a tribunal, the tribunal shall direct the absolute discharge of the patient if satisfied—

(a) as to the matters mentioned in paragraph (b)(i) or (ii) of section 72(1) above ; and

(b) that it is not appropriate for the patient to remain liable to be recalled to hospital for further treatment.

(2) Where in the case of any such patient as is mentioned in subsection (1) above the tribunal are satisfied as to the matters referred to in paragraph (a) of that subsection but not as to the matter referred to in paragraph (b) of that subsection the tribunal shall direct the conditional discharge of the patient.

(3) Where a patient is absolutely discharged under this section he shall thereupon cease to be liable to be detained by virtue of the relevant hospital order, and the restriction order shall cease to have effect accordingly.

(4) Where a patient is conditionally discharged under this section—

(a) he may be recalled by the Secretary of State under subsection (3) of section 42 above as if he had been conditionally discharged under subsection (2) of that section; and

(b) the patient shall comply with such conditions (if any) as may be imposed at the time of discharge by the tribunal or at any subsequent time by the Secretary of State.

(5) The Secretary of State may from time to time vary any condition imposed (whether by the tribunal or by him) under subsection (4) above.

(6) Where a restriction order in respect of a patient ceases to have effect after he has been conditionally discharged under this section the patient shall, unless previously recalled, be deemed to be absolutely discharged on the date when the order ceases to have effect and shall cease to be liable to be detained by virtue of the relevant hospital order.

(7) A tribunal may defer a direction for the conditional discharge of a patient until such arrangements as appear to the tribunal to be necessary for that purpose have been made to their satisfaction; and where by virtue of any such deferment no direction has been given on an application or reference before the time when the patient's case comes before the tribunal on a subsequent application or reference, the previous application or reference shall be treated as one on which no direction under this section can be given.

(8) This section is without prejudice to section 42 above.

## 74 Restricted patients subject to restriction directions

(1) Where an application to a Mental Health Review Tribunal is made by a restricted patient who is subject to a restriction direction, or where the case of such a patient is referred to such a tribunal, the tribunal—

(a) shall notify the Secretary of State whether, in their opinion, the patient would, if subject to a restriction order, be entitled to be absolutely or conditionally discharged under section 73 above; and

(b) if they notify him that the patient would be entitled to be conditionally discharged, may recommend that in the event of his not being discharged under this section he should continue to be detained in hospital.

(2) If in the case of a patient not falling within subsection (4) below—

(a) the tribunal notify the Secretary of State that the patient would be entitled to be absolutely or conditionally discharged; and

(b) within the period of 90 days beginning with the date of that notification the Secretary of State gives notice to the tribunal that the patient may be so discharged,

the tribunal shall direct the absolute or, as the case may be, the conditional discharge of the patient.

(3) Where a patient continues to be liable to be detained in a hospital at the end of the period referred to in subsection (2)(b) above because the Secretary of State has not given the notice there mentioned, the managers of the hospital shall, unless the tribunal have made a recommendation under subsection (1)(b) above, transfer the patient to a prison or other institution in which he might have been detained if he had not been removed to hospital, there to be dealt with as if he had not been so removed.

(4) If, in the case of a patient who is subject to a transfer direction under section 48 above, the tribunal notify the Secretary of State that the patient would be entitled to be absolutely or conditionally discharged, the Secretary of State shall, unless the tribunal have made a recommendation under subsection (1)(b) above, by warrant direct that the patient be remitted to a prison or other institution in which he might have been detained if he had not been removed to hospital, there to be dealt with as if he had not been so removed.

(5) Where a patient is transferred or remitted under subsection (3) or (4) above the relevant transfer direction and the restriction direction shall cease to have effect on his arrival in the prison or other institution.

(6) Subsections (3) to (8) of section 73 above shall have effect in relation to this section as they have effect in relation to that section, taking references to the relevant hospital order and the restriction order as references to the transfer direction and the restriction direction.

(7) This section is without prejudice to sections 50 to 53 above in their application to patients who are not discharged under this section.

### 75 Applications and references concerning conditionally discharged restricted patients

(1) Where a restricted patient has been conditionally discharged under section 42(2), 73 or 74 above and is subsequently recalled to hospital—

(a) the Secretary of State shall, within one month of the day on which the patient returns or is returned to hospital, refer his case to a Mental Health Review Tribunal; and

(b) section 70 above shall apply to the patient as if the relevant hospital order or transfer direction had been made on that day.

(2) Where a restricted patient has been conditionally discharged as aforesaid but has not been recalled to hospital he may apply to a Mental Health Review Tribunal—

(a) in the period between the expiration of 12 months and the expiration of two years beginning with the date on which he was conditionally discharged; and

(b) in any subsequent period of two years.

(3) Sections 73 and 74 above shall not apply to an application under subsection (2) above but on any such application the tribunal may—

(a) vary any condition to which the patient is subject in connection with his discharge or impose any condition which might have been imposed in connection therewith ; or

(b) direct that the restriction order or restriction direction to which he is subject shall cease to have effect;

and if the tribunal give a direction under paragraph (b) above the patient shall cease to be liable to be detained by virtue of the relevant hospital order or transfer direction.

### *General*

## 76 Visiting and examination of patients

(1) For the purpose of advising whether an application to a Mental Health Review Tribunal should be made by or in respect of a patient who is liable to be detained or subject to guardianship under Part II of this Act or of furnishing information as to the condition of a patient for the purposes of such an application, any registered medical practitioner authorised by or on behalf of the patient or other person who is entitled to make or has made the application—

(a) may at any reasonable time visit the patient and examine him in private, and

(b) may require the production of and inspect any records relating to the detention or treatment of the patient in any hospital.

(2) Section 32 above shall apply for the purposes of this section as it applies for the purposes of Part II of this Act.

## 77 General provisions concerning tribunal applications

(1) No application shall be made to a Mental Health Review Tribunal by or in respect of a patient except in such cases and at such times as are expressly provided by this Act.

(2) Where under this Act any person is authorised to make an application to a Mental Health Review Tribunal within a specified period, not more than one such application shall be made by that person within that period but for that purpose there shall be disregarded any application which is withdrawn in accordance with rules made under section 78 below.

(3) Subject to subsection (4) below an application to a Mental Health Review Tribunal authorised to be made by or in respect of a patient under this Act shall be made by notice in writing addressed to the tribunal for the area in which the hospital in which the patient is detained is situated or in which the patient is residing under guardianship as the case may be.

(4) Any application under section 75(2) above shall be made to the tribunal for the area in which the patient resides.

## 78 Procedure of tribunals

(1) The Lord Chancellor may make rules with respect to the making of applications to Mental Health Review Tribunals and with respect to the proceedings of such tribunals and matters incidental to or consequential on such proceedings.

(2) Rules made under this section may in particular make provision—

(a) for enabling a tribunal, or the chairman of a tribunal, to postpone the consideration of any application by or in respect of a patient, or of any such application of any specified class, until the expiration of such period (not exceeding 12 months) as may be specified in the rules from the date on which an application by or in respect of the same patient was last considered and determined by that or any other tribunal under this Act;

(b) for the transfer of proceedings from one tribunal to another in any case where, after the making of the application, the patient is removed out of the area of the tribunal to which it was made;

(c) for restricting the persons qualified to serve as members of a tribunal for the consideration of any application, or of an application of any specified class;

(d) for enabling a tribunal to dispose of an application without a formal hearing where such a hearing is not requested by the applicant or it appears to the tribunal that such a hearing would be detrimental to the health of the patient;

(e) for enabling a tribunal to exclude members of the public, or any specified class of members of the public, from any proceedings of the tribunal, or to prohibit the publication of reports of any such proceedings or the names of any persons concerned in such proceedings;

(f) for regulating the circumstances in which, and the persons by whom, applicants and patients in respect of whom applications are made to a tribunal may, if not desiring to conduct their own case, be represented for the purposes of those applications ;

(g) for regulating the methods by which information relevant to an application may be obtained by or furnished to the tribunal, and in particular for authorising the members of a tribunal, or any one or more of them, to visit and interview in private any patient by or in respect of whom an application has been made;

(h) for making available to any applicant, and to any" patient in respect of whom an application is made to a tribunal, copies of any documents obtained by or furnished to the tribunal in connection with the application, and a statement of the substance of any oral information so obtained or furnished except where the tribunal considers it undesirable in the interests of the patient or for other special reasons ;

(i) for requiring a tribunal, if so requested in accordance with the rules, to furnish such statements of the reasons for any decision given by the tribunal as may be prescribed by the rules, subject to any provision made by the rules for withholding such a statement from a patient or any other person in cases where the tribunal considers that furnishing it would be undesirable in the interests of the patient or for other special reasons;

(j) for conferring on the tribunals such ancillary powers as the Lord Chancellor thinks necessary for the purposes of the exercise of their functions under this Act;

(k) for enabling any functions of a tribunal which relate to matters preliminary or incidental to an application to be performed by the chairman of the tribunal.

(3) Subsections (1) and (2) above apply in relation to references to Mental Health Review Tribunals as they apply in relation to applications to such tribunals by or in respect of patients.

(4) Rules under this section may make provision as to the procedure to be adopted in cases concerning restricted patients and, in particular—

(a) for restricting the persons qualified to serve as president of a tribunal for the consideration of an application or reference relating to a restricted patient;

(b) for the transfer of proceedings from one tribunal to another in any case where, after the making of a reference or application in accordance with section 71(4) or 77(4) above, the patient ceases to reside in the area of the tribunal to which the reference or application was made.

(5) Rules under this section may be so framed as to apply to all applications or references or to applications or references of any specified class and may make different provision in relation to different cases.

(6) Any functions conferred on the chairman of a Mental Health Review Tribunal by rules under this section may, if for any reason he is unable to act, be exercised by another member of that tribunal appointed by him for the purpose.

(7) A Mental Health Review Tribunal may pay allowances in respect of travelling expenses, subsistence and loss of earnings to any person attending the tribunal as an applicant or witness, to the patient who is the subject of the proceedings if he attends otherwise than as the applicant or a witness and to any person (other than counsel or a solicitor) who attends as the representative of an applicant.

(8) A Mental Health Review Tribunal may, and if so required by the High Court shall, state in the form of a special case for determination by the High Court any question of law which may arise before them.

(9) The Arbitration Act 1950 shall not apply to any proceedings before a Mental Health Review Tribunal except so far as any provisions of that Act may be applied, with or without modifications, by rules made under this section.

### 79 Interpretation of Part V

(1) In this Part of this Act " restricted patient" means a patient who is subject to a restriction order or restriction direction and this Part of this Act shall, subject to the provisions of this section, have effect in relation to any person who—

(a) is subject to a direction which by virtue of section 46(3) above has the same effect as a hospital order and a restriction order; or

(b) is treated as subject to a hospital order and a restriction order by virtue of an order under section 5(1) of the Criminal Procedure (Insanity) Act 1964 or section 6 or 14(1) of the Criminal Appeal Act 1968 ; or

(c) is treated as subject to a hospital order and a restriction order or to a transfer direction and a restriction direction by virtue of section 82(2) or 85(2) below or section 73(2) of the Mental Health (Scotland) Act 1960,

as it has effect in relation to a restricted patient.

(2) Subject to the following provisions of this section, in this Part of this Act " the relevant hospital order " and " the relevant transfer direction ", in relation to a restricted patient, mean the hospital order or transfer direction by virtue of which he is liable to be detained in a hospital.

(3) In the case of a person within paragraph (a) of subsection (1) above, references in this Part of this Act to the relevant hospital order or restriction order shall be construed as references to the direction referred to in that paragraph.

(4) In the case of a person within paragraph (b) of subsection (1) above, references in this Part of this Act to the relevant hospital order or restriction order shall be construed as references to the order under the provisions mentioned in that paragraph.

(5) In the case of a person within paragraph (c) of subsection (1) above, references in this Part of this Act to the relevant hospital order, the relevant transfer direction, the restriction order or the restriction direction or to a transfer direction under section 48 above shall be construed as references to the hospital order, transfer direction, restriction order, restriction direction or transfer direction under that section to which that person is treated as subject by virtue of the provisions mentioned in that paragraph.

(6) In this Part of this Act, unless the context otherwise requires, " hospital" means a hospital within the meaning of Part II of this Act.

## PART VI

### REMOVAL AND RETURN OF PATIENTS WITHIN UNITED KINGDOM, ETC.

*Removal to Scotland*

### 80 Removal of patients to Scotland

(1) if it appears to the Secretary of State, in the case of a patient who is for the time being liable to be detained or subject to guardianship under this Act (otherwise than by virtue of section 35, 36 or 38 above), that it is in the interests of the patient to remove him to Scotland, and that arrangements have been made for admitting him to a hospital or, as the case may be, for receiving him into guardianship there, the Secretary of State may authorise his removal to Scotland and may give any necessary directions for his conveyance to his destination.

(2) Subject to the provisions of subsection (4) below, where a patient liable to be detained under this Act by virtue of an application, order or direction under any enactment in force in England and Wales is removed under this section and admitted to a hospital in Scotland, he shall be treated as if on the date of his admission he had been so admitted in pursuance of an application forwarded to the Health Board responsible for the administration of the hospital, or an order or direction made or given, on that date under the corresponding enactment in Scotland, and, where he is subject to a restriction order or restriction direction under any enactment in this Act, as if he were subject to an order or direction under the corresponding enactment in force in Scotland.

(3) Where a patient subject to guardianship under this Act by virtue of an application, order or direction under any enactment in force in England and Wales is removed under this section and received into guardianship in Scotland, he shall be treated as if on the date on which he arrives at the place where he is to reside he had been so received in pursuance of an application, order or direction under the corresponding enactment in force in Scotland, and as if the application had been forwarded or, as the case may be, the order or direction had been made or given on that date.

(4) Where a person removed under this section was immediately before his removal liable to be detained by virtue of an application for admission for assessment under this Act, he shall, on his admission to a hospital in Scotland, be treated as if he had been admitted to the hospital in pursuance of an emergency recommendation under the Mental Health (Scotland) Act 1960 made on the date of his admission.

(5) Where a patient removed under this section was immediately before his removal liable to be detained under this Act by virtue of a transfer direction given while he was serving a sentence of imprisonment (within the meaning of section 47(5) above) imposed by a court in England and Wales, he shall be treated as if the sentence had been imposed by a court in Scotland.

(6) Where a person removed under this section was immediately before his removal subject to a restriction order or restriction direction of limited duration, the order or direction restricting his discharge to which he is subject by virtue of subsection (2)

above shall expire on the date on which the restriction order or restriction direction would have expired if he had not been so removed.

(7) In this section "hospital" has the same meaning as in the Mental Health (Scotland) Act 1960.

*Removal to and from Northern Ireland*

## 81 Removal of patients to Northern Ireland

(1) If it appears to the Secretary of State, in the case of a patient who is for the time being liable to be detained or subject to guardianship under this Act (otherwise than by virtue of section 35, 36 or 38 above), that it is in the interests of the patient to remove him to Northern Ireland, and that arrangements have been made for admitting him to a hospital or, as the case may be, for receiving him into guardianship there, the Secretary of State may authorise his removal to Northern Ireland and may give any necessary directions for his conveyance to his destination.

(2) Subject to the provisions of subsections (4) and (5) below, where a patient liable to be detained under lids Act by virtue of an application, order or direction under any enactment in force in England and Wales is removed under this section and admitted to a hospital in Northern Ireland, he shall be treated as if on the date of his admission he had been so admitted in pursuance of an application made, or an order or direction made or given, on that date under the corresponding enactment in force in Northern Ireland, and, where he is subject to a restriction order or restriction direction under any enactment in this Act, as if he were subject to an order or direction under the corresponding enactment in force in Northern Ireland.

(3) Where a patient subject to guardianship under this Act by virtue of an application, order or direction under any enactment in force in England and Wales is removed under this section and received into guardianship in Northern Ireland, he shall be treated as if on the date on which he arrives at the place where he is to reside he had been so received in pursuance of an application, order or direction under the corresponding enactment in force in Northern Ireland, and as if the application had been accepted or, as the case may be, the order or direction had been made or given on that date.

(4) Where a person removed under this section was immediately before his removal liable to be detained by virtue of an application for admission for assessment under this Act, he shall, on his admission to a hospital in Northern Ireland, be treated as if he had been admitted to the hospital in pursuance of an application for admission under section 12 of the Mental Health Act (Northern Ireland) 1961 made on the date of his admission.

(5) Where a person removed under this section was immediately before his removal liable to be detained by virtue of an application for admission for treatment under this Act, he shall, on his admission to a hospital in Northern Ireland, be treated as if—

- (a) he had been admitted to the hospital in pursuance of an application for admission under section 12 of the Mental Health Act (Northern Ireland) 1961 made on the date of his admission; and
- (b) a medical report under section 19 of that Act had been made in respect of him on that date.

(6) Where a patient removed under this section was immediately before his removal liable to be detained under this Act by virtue of a transfer direction given while he was serving a sentence of imprisonment (within the meaning of section 47(5) above)

imposed by a court in England and Wales, he shall be treated as if the sentence had been imposed by a court in Northern Ireland.

(7) Where a person removed under this section was immediately before his removal subject to a restriction order or restriction direction of limited duration, the order or direction restricting his discharge to which he is subject by virtue of subsection (2) above shall expire on the date on which the restriction order or restriction direction would have expired if he had not been so removed.

(8) In this section " hospital" has the same meaning as in the Mental Health Act (Northern Ireland) 1961.

## 82 Removal to England and Wales of patients from Northern Ireland

(1) If it appears to the responsible authority, in the case of a patient who is for the time being liable to be detained or subject to guardianship under the Mental Health Act (Northern Ireland) 1961, that it is in the interests of the patient to remove him to England and Wales, and that arrangements have been made for admitting him to a hospital or, as the case may be, for receiving him into guardianship there, the responsible authority may authorise his removal to England and Wales and may give any necessary directions for his conveyance to his destination.

(2) Subject to the provisions of subsection (4) below, where a patient who is liable to be detained under the said Act of 1961 by virtue of an application, order or direction under any enactment in force in Northern Ireland is removed under this section and admitted to a hospital in England and Wales, he shall be treated as if on the date of his admission he had been so admitted in pursuance of an application made, or an order or direction made or given, on that date under the corresponding enactment in force in England and Wales and, where he is subject to an order or direction under any enactment in the said Act of 1961 restricting his discharge, as if he were subject to a restriction order or restriction direction.

(3) Where a patient subject to guardianship under the said Act of 1961 by virtue of an application, order or direction under any enactment in force in Northern Ireland is removed under this section and received into guardianship in England and Wales, he shall be treated as if on the date on which he arrives at the place where he is to reside he had been so received in pursuance of an application, order or direction under the corresponding enactment in force in England and Wales and as if the application had been accepted or, as the case may be, the order or direction had been made or given on that date.

(4) Where a person removed under this section was immediately before his removal liable to be detained by virtue of an application for admission under section 12 of the said Act of 1961 he shall—

(a) if a report under section 19 of that Act has not been made in respect of him, be treated, on his admission to a hospital in England and Wales, as if he had been admitted to the hospital in pursuance of an application for admission for assessment made on the date of his admission;

(b) if a report under the said section 19 has been made in respect of him, be treated, on his admission to a hospital in England and Wales, as if he had been admitted to the hospital in pursuance of an application for admission for treatment made on the date of his admission.

(5) Where a patient removed under this section was immediately before his removal liable to be detained under the said Act of 1961 by virtue of a transfer direction given while he was serving a sentence of imprisonment (within the meaning of section 58(6) of that Act) imposed by a court in Northern Ireland, he shall be treated as if the sentence had been imposed by a court in England and Wales.

(6) Where a person removed under this section was immediately before his removal subject to an order or direction restricting his discharge, being an order or direction of limited duration, the restriction order or restriction direction to which he is subject by virtue of subsection (2) above shall expire on the date on which the first-mentioned order or direction would have expired if he had not been so removed.

(7) In this section " the responsible authority " means the Department of Health and Social Services for Northern Ireland or, in relation to a patient who is subject to an order or direction restricting his discharge, the Secretary of State.

*Removal to and from Channel Islands and Isle of Man*

### 83 Removal of patients to Channel Islands or Isle of Man

If it appears to the Secretary of State, in the case of a patient who is for the time being liable to be detained or subject to guardianship under this Act (otherwise than by virtue of section 35, 36 or 38 above), that it is in the interests of the patient to remove him to any of the Channel Islands or to the Isle of Man, and that arrangements have been made for admitting him to a hospital or, as the case may be, for receiving him into guardianship there, the Secretary of State may authorise his removal to the island in question and may give any necessary directions for his conveyance to his destination.

### 84 Removal to England and Wales of offenders found insane in Channel Islands and Isle of Man

(1) The Secretary of State may by warrant direct that any offender found by a court in any of the Channel Islands or in the Isle of Man to be insane or to have been insane at the time of the alleged offence, and ordered to be detained during Her Majesty's pleasure, be removed to a hospital in England and Wales.

(2) A patient removed under subsection (1) above shall, on his reception into the hospital in England and Wales, be treated as if he had been removed to that hospital in pursuance of a direction under section 46 above.

(3) The Secretary of State may by warrant direct that any patient removed under this section from any of the Channel Islands or from the Isle of Man be returned to the island from which he was so removed, there to be dealt with according to law in all respects as if he had not been removed under this section.

### 85 Patients removed from Channel Islands or Isle of Man

(1) This section applies to any patient who is removed to England and Wales from any of the Channel Islands or the Isle of Man under a provision corresponding to section 83 above and who immediately before his removal was liable to be detained or subject to guardianship in the island in question under a provision corresponding to an enactment contained in this Act (other than section 35, 36 or 38 above).

(2) Where the patient is admitted to a hospital in England and Wales he shall be treated as if on the date of his admission he had been so admitted in pursuance of an application made, or an order or direction made or given, on that date under the corresponding enactment contained in this Act and, where he is subject to an order or direction restricting his discharge, as if he were subject to a restriction order or restriction direction.

(3) Where the patient is received into guardianship in England and Wales, he shall be treated as if on the date on which he arrives at the place where he is to reside he had been so received in pursuance of an application, order or direction under the corresponding enactment contained in this Act and as if the application had been accepted or, as the case may be, the order or direction had been made or given on that date.

(4) Where the patient was immediately before his removal liable to be detained by virtue of a transfer direction given while he was serving a sentence of imprisonment imposed by a court in the island in question, he shall be treated as if the sentence had been imposed by a court in England and Wales.

(5) Where the patient was immediately before his removal subject to an order or direction restricting his discharge, being an order or direction of limited duration, the restriction order or restriction direction to which he is subject by virtue of subsection (2) above shall expire on the date on which the first-mentioned order or direction would have expired if he had not been removed.

(6) While being conveyed to the hospital referred to in subsection (2) or, as the case may be, the place referred to in subsection (3) above, the patient shall be deemed to be in legal custody, and section 138 below shall apply to him as if he were in legal custody by virtue of section 137 below.

(7) In the case of a patient removed from the Isle of Man the reference in subsection (4) above to a person serving a sentence of imprisonment includes a reference to a person detained as mentioned in section 60(6)(a) of the Mental Health Act 1974 (an Act of Tynwald).

*Removal of aliens*

## 86 Removal of alien patients

(1) This section applies to any patient who is neither a British citizen nor a Commonwealth citizen having the right of abode in the United Kingdom by virtue of section 2(1)(b) of the Immigration Act 1971, being a patient who is receiving treatment for mental illness as an in-patient in a hospital in England and Wales or a hospital within the meaning of the Mental Health Act (Northern Ireland) 1961 and is detained pursuant to—

- (a) an application for admission for treatment or an application under section 12 of the said Act of 1961;
- (b) a hospital order under section 37 above or section 48 of the said Act of 1961; or
- (c) an order or direction under this Act (other than under section 35, 36 or 38 above) or the said Act of 1961 having the same effect as such a hospital order.

(2) If it appears to the Secretary of State that proper arrangements have been made for the removal of a patient to whom this section applies to a country or territory outside the United Kingdom, the Isle of Man and the Channel Islands and for his care or treatment

there and that it is in the interests of the patient to remove him, the Secretary of State may, subject to subsection (3) below—

(a) by warrant authorise the removal of the patient from the place where he is receiving treatment as mentioned in subsection (1) above, and

(b) give such directions as the Secretary of State thinks fit for the conveyance of the patient to his destination in that country or territory and for his detention in any place or on board any ship or aircraft until his arrival at any specified port or place in any such country or territory.

(3) The Secretary of State shall not exercise his powers under subsection (2) above in the case of any patient except with the approval of a Mental Health Review Tribunal or, as the case may be, of the Mental Health Review Tribunal for Northern Ireland.

*Return of patients absent without leave*

### 87 Patients absent from hospitals in Northern Ireland

(1) Any person who—

(a) under section 30 or section 108 of the Mental Health Act (Northern Ireland) 1961 (which provide, respectively, for the retaking of patients absent without leave and for the retaking of patients escaping from custody); or

(b) under the said section 30 as applied by section 34 of the said Act of 1961 (which makes special provision as to persons sentenced to imprisonment),

may be taken into custody in Northern Ireland, may be taken into custody in, and returned to Northern Ireland from, England and Wales by an approved social worker, by any constable or by any person authorised by or by virtue of the said Act of 1961 to take him into custody.

(2) This section does not apply to any person who is subject to guardianship.

### 88 Patients absent from hospitals in England and Wales

(1) Subject to the provisions of this section, any person who, under section 18 above or section 138 below or under the said section 18 as applied by section 22 above, may be taken into custody in England and Wales may be taken into custody in, and returned to England and Wales from, any other part of the United Kingdom or the Channel Islands or the Isle of Man.

(2) For the purposes of the enactments referred to in subsection (1) above, in their application by virtue of this section to Scotland, Northern Ireland, the Channel Islands or the Isle of Man, the expression "constable" includes a Scottish constable, an officer or constable of the Royal Ulster Constabulary, a member of the police in Jersey, an officer of police within the meaning of section 43 of the Larceny (Guernsey) Law 1958 or any corresponding law for the time being in force, or a constable in the Isle of Man, as the case may be.

(3) For the purposes of the said enactments in their application by virtue of this section to Scotland or Northern Ireland, any reference to an approved social worker shall be construed as including a reference—

(a) in Scotland, to any mental health officer within the meaning of the Mental Health (Scotland) Act 1960;

(b) in Northern Ireland, to any social worker within the meaning of the Mental Health Act (Northern Ireland) 1961.

(4) This section does not apply to any person who is subject to guardianship.

### 89 Patients absent from hospitals in the Channel Islands or Isle of Man

(1) Any person who under any provision corresponding to section 18 above or 138 below may be taken into custody in any of the Channel Islands or the Isle of Man may be taken into custody in, and returned to the island in question from, England and Wales by an approved social worker or a constable.

(2) This section does not apply to any person who is subject to guardianship.

*General*

### 90 Regulations for purposes of Part VI

Section 32 above shall have effect as if references in that section to Part II of this Act included references to this Part of this Act and to Part VI of the Mental Health (Scotland) Act 1960, so far as those Parts apply to patients removed to England and Wales thereunder.

### 91 General provisions as to patients removed from England and Wales

(1) Subject to subsection (2) below, where a patient liable to be detained or subject to guardianship by virtue of an application, order or direction under Part II or III of this Act (other than section 35, 36 or 38 above) is removed from England and Wales in pursuance of arrangements under this Part of this Act, the application, order or direction shall cease to have effect when he is duly received into a hospital or other institution, or placed under guardianship, in pursuance of those arrangements.

(2) Where the Secretary of State exercises his powers under section 86(2) above in respect of a patient who is detained pursuant to a hospital order under section 37 above and in respect of whom a restriction order is in force, those orders shall continue in force so as to apply to the patient if he returns to England and Wales at any time before the end of the period for which those orders would have continued in force.

### 92 Interpretation of Part VI

(1) References in this Part of this Act to a hospital, being a hospital in England and Wales, shall be construed as references to a hospital within the meaning of Part II of this Act.

(2) Where a patient is treated by virtue of this Part of this Act as if he had been removed to a hospital in England and Wales in pursuance of a direction under Part III of this Act, that direction shall be deemed to have been given on the date of his reception into the hospital.

(3) A patient removed to England and Wales under this Part of this Act or under Part VI of the Mental Health (Scotland) Act 1960 shall be treated for the purposes of this Act as suffering from such form of mental disorder as may be recorded in his case in pursuance of regulations made by virtue of section 90 above, and references in this Act to the form or forms of mental disorder specified in the relevant application, order

or direction shall be construed as including references to the form or forms of mental disorder so recorded.

## PART VII

### MANAGEMENT OF PROPERTY AND AFFAIRS OF PATIENTS

#### 93 Judicial authorities and Court of Protection

(1) The Lord Chancellor shall from time to time nominate one or more judges of the Supreme Court (in this Act referred to as " nominated judges ") to act for the purposes of this Part of this Act.

(2) There shall continue to be an office of the Supreme Court, called the Court of Protection, for the protection and management, as provided by this Part of this Act, of the property and affairs of persons under disability ; and there shall continue to be a Master of the Court of Protection appointed by the Lord Chancellor under section 89 of the Supreme Court Act 1981.

(3) The Master of the Court of Protection shall take the oath of allegiance and judicial oath in the presence of the Lord Chancellor; and the Promissory Oaths Act 1868 shall have effect as if the officers named in the Second Part of the Schedule to that Act included the Master of the Court of Protection.

(4) The Lord Chancellor may nominate other officers of the Court of Protection (in this Part of this Act referred to as " nominated officers ") to act for the purposes of this Part of this Act.

#### 94 Exercise of judge's functions: " the patient "

(1) The functions expressed to be conferred by this Part of this Act on the judge shall be exercisable by the Lord Chancellor or by any nominated judge, and shall also be exercisable by the Master of the Court of Protection or by any nominated officer, but—

- (a) in the case of the Master or any nominated officer, subject to any express provision to the contrary in this Part of this Act or any rules made under this Part of this Act,
- (b) in the case of any nominated officer, subject to any directions of the Master and so far only as may be provided by the instrument by which he is nominated;

and references in this Part of this Act to the judge shall be construed accordingly.

(2) The functions of the judge under this Part of this Act shall be exercisable where, after considering medical evidence, he is satisfied that a person is incapable, by reason of mental disorder, of managing and administering his property and affairs; and a person as to whom the judge is so satisfied is referred to in this Part of this Act as a patient.

#### 95 General functions of the judge with respect to property and affairs of patient

(1) The judge may, with respect to the property and affairs of a patient, do or secure the doing of all such things as appear necessary or expedient—

- (a) for the maintenance or other benefit of the patient,
- (b) for the maintenance or other benefit of members of the patient's family,

(c) for making provision for other persons or purposes for whom or which the patient might be expected to provide if he were not mentally disordered, or

(d) otherwise for administering the patient's affairs.

(2) In the exercise of the powers conferred by this section regard shall be had first of all to the requirements of the patient, and the rules of law which restricted the enforcement by a creditor of rights against property under the control of the judge in lunacy shall apply to property under the control of the judge ; but, subject to the foregoing provisions of this subsection, the judge shall, in administering a patient's affairs, have regard to the interests of creditors and also to the desirability of making provision for obligations of the patient notwithstanding that they may not be legally enforceable.

### 96 Powers of the judge as to patient's property and affairs

(1) Without prejudice to the generality of section 95 above, the judge shall have power to make such orders and give such directions and authorities as he thinks fit for the purposes of that section and in particular may for those purposes make orders or give directions or authorities for—

(a) the control (with or without the transfer or vesting of property or the payment into or lodgment in the Supreme Court of money or securities) and management of any property of the patient;

(b) the sale, exchange, charging or other disposition of or dealing with any property of the patient;

(c) the acquisition of any property in the name or on behalf of the patient;

(d) the settlement of any property of the patient, or the gift of any property of the patient to any such persons or for any such purposes as are mentioned in paragraphs (b) and (c) of section 95(1) above ;

(e) the execution for the patient of a will making any pro vision (whether by way of disposing of property or exercising a power or otherwise) which could be made by a will executed by the patient if he were not mentally disordered;

(f) the carrying on by a suitable person of any profession, trade or business of the patient;

(g) the dissolution of a partnership of which the patient is a member;

(h) the carrying out of any contract entered into by the patient;

(j) the conduct of legal proceedings in the name of the patient or on his behalf ;

(j) the reimbursement out of the property of the patient, with or without interest, of money applied by any person either in payment of the patient's debts (whether legally enforceable or not) or for the maintenance or other benefit of the patient or members of his family or in making provision for other persons or purposes for whom or which he might be expected to provide if he were not mentally disordered;

(k) the exercise of any power (including a power to consent) vested in the patient, whether beneficially, or as guardian or trustee, or otherwise.

(2) If under subsection (1) above provision is made for the settlement of any property of a patient, or the exercise of a power vested in a patient of appointing trustees or retiring from a trust, the judge may also make as respects the property settled or trust property such consequential vesting or other orders as the case may require, including (in the case of the exercise of such a power) any order which could have been made in such a case under Part IV of the Trustee Act 1925.

(3) Where under this section a settlement has been made of any property of a patient, and the Lord Chancellor or a nominated judge is satisfied, at any time before the death of the patient, that any material fact was not disclosed when the settlement was made, or that there has been any substantial change in circumstances, he may by order vary the settlement in such manner as he thinks fit, and give any consequential directions.

(4) The power of the judge to make or give an order, direction or authority for the execution of a will for a patient—

(a) shall not be exercisable at any time when the patient is a minor, and

(b) shall not be exercised unless the judge has reason to believe that the patient is incapable of making a valid will for himself.

(5) The powers of a patient as patron of a benefice shall be exercisable by the Lord Chancellor only.

**97 Supplementary provisions as to wills executed under s. 96**

(1) Where under section 96(1) above the judge makes or gives an order, direction or authority requiring or authorising a person (in this section referred to as " the authorised person ") to execute a will for a patient, any will executed in pursuance of that order, direction or authority shall be expressed to be signed by the patient acting by the authorised person, and shall be—

(a) signed by the authorised person with the name of the patient, and with his own name, in the presence of two or more witnesses present at the same time, and

(b) attested and subscribed by those witnesses in the presence of the authorised person, and

(c) sealed with the official seal of the Court of Protection.

(2) The Wills Act 1837 shall have effect in relation to any such will as if it were signed by the patient by his own hand, except that in relation to any such will—

(a) section 9 of that Act (which makes provision as to the signing and attestation of wills) shall not apply, and

(b) in the subsequent provisions of that Act any reference to execution in the manner required by the previous provisions of that Act shall be construed as a reference to execution in the maimer required by subsection (1) above.

(3) Subject to the following provisions of this section, any such will executed in accordance with subsection (1) above shall have the same effect for all purposes as if the patient were capable of making a valid will and the will had been executed by him in the manner required by the Wills Act 1837.

(4) So much of subsection (3) above as provides for such a will to have effect as if the patient were capable of making a valid will—

(a) shall not have effect in relation to such a will in so far as it disposes of any immovable property, other than immovable property in England or Wales, and

(b) where at the time when such a will is executed the patient is domiciled in Scotland or Northern Ireland or in a country or territory outside the United Kingdom, shall not have effect in relation to that will in so far as it relates to any other property or matter, except any property or matter in respect of which, under the law of his domicile, any question of his testamentary capacity would fall to be determined in accordance with the law of England and Wales.

## 98 Judge's powers in cases of emergency

Where it is represented to the judge, and he has reason to believe, that a person may be incapable, by reason of mental disorder, of managing and administering his property and affairs, and the judge is of the opinion that it is necessary to make immediate provision for any of the matters referred to in section 95 above, then pending the determination of the question whether that person is so incapable the judge may exercise in relation to the property and affairs of that person any of the powers conferred on him in relation to the property and affairs of a patient by this Part of this Act so far as is requisite for enabling that provision to be made.

## 99 Power to appoint receiver

(1) The judge may by order appoint as receiver for a patient a person specified in the order or the holder for the time being of an office so specified.

(2) A person appointed as receiver for a patient shall do all such things in relation to the property and affairs of the patient as the judge, in the exercise of the powers conferred on him by sections 95 and 96 above, orders or directs him to do and may do any such thing in relation to the property and affairs of the patient as the judge, in the exercise of those powers, authorises him to do.

(3) A receiver appointed for any person shall be discharged by order of the judge on the judge being satisfied that mat person has become capable of managing and administering his property and affairs, and may be discharged by order of the judge at any time if the judge considers it expedient to do so; and a receiver shall be discharged (without any order) on the death of the patient.

## 100 Vesting of stock in curator appointed outside England and Wales

(1) Where the judge is satisfied—

- (a) that under the law prevailing in a place outside England and Wales a person has been appointed to exercise powers with respect to the property or affairs of any other person on the ground (however formulated) that that other person is incapable, by reason of mental disorder, of managing and administering his property and affairs, and
- (b) that having regard to the nature of the appointment and to the circumstances of the case it is expedient that the judge should exercise his powers under this section,

the judge may direct any stock standing in the name of the said other person or the right to receive the dividends from the stock to be transferred into the name of the person so appointed or otherwise dealt with as requested by that person, and may give such directions as the judge thinks fit for dealing with accrued dividends from the stock.

(2) In this section " stock " includes shares and also any fund, annuity or security transferable in the books kept by any body corporate or unincorporated company or society, or by an instrument of transfer either alone or accompanied by other formalities, and " dividends " shall be construed accordingly.

## 101 Preservation of interests in patient's property

(1) Where any property of a person has been disposed of under this Part of this Act, and under his will or his intestacy, or by any gift perfected or nomination taking effect on

his death, any other person would have taken an interest in the property but for the disposal—

(a) he shall take the same interest, if and so far as circumstances allow, in any property belonging to the estate of the deceased which represents the property disposed of; and

(b) if the property disposed of was real property any property representing it shall so long as it remains part of his estate be treated as if it were real property.

(2) The judge, in ordering, directing or authorising under this Part of this Act any disposal of property which apart from this section would result in the conversion of personal property into real property, may direct that the property representing the property disposed of shall, so long as it remains the property of the patient or forms part of his estate, be treated as if it were personal property.

(3) References in subsections (1) and (2) above to the disposal of property are references to—

(a) the sale, exchange, charging or other dealing (otherwise than by will) with property other than money,

(b) the removal of property from one place to another,

(c) the application of money in acquiring property, or

(d) the transfer of money from one account to another;

and references to property representing property disposed of shall be construed accordingly and as including the result of successive disposals.

(4) The judge may give such directions as appear to him necessary or expedient for the purpose of facilitating the operation of subsection (1) above, including the carrying of money to a separate account and the transfer of property other than money.

(5) Where the judge has ordered, directed or authorised the expenditure of money for the carrying out of permanent improvements on, or otherwise for the permanent benefit of, any property of the patient, he may order that the whole or any part of the money expended or to be expended shall be a charge upon the property, whether without interest or with interest at a specified rate; and an order under this subsection may provide for excluding or restricting the operation of subsection (1) above.

(6) A charge under subsection (5) above may be made in favour of such person as may be just, and in particular, where the money charged is paid out of the patient's general estate, may be made in favour of a person as trustee for the patient; but no charge under that subsection shall confer any right of sale or foreclosure during the lifetime of the patient.

### 102 Lord Chancellor's Visitors

(1) There shall continue to be the following panels of Lord Chancellor's Visitors of patients constituted in accordance with this section, namely—

(a) a panel of Medical Visitors ;

(b) a panel of Legal Visitors; and

(c) a panel of General Visitors (being Visitors who are not required by this section to possess either a medical or legal qualification for appointment).

(2) Each panel shall consist of persons appointed to it by the Lord Chancellor, the appointment of each person being for such term and subject to such conditions as the Lord Chancellor may determine.

(3) A person shall not be qualified to be appointed—

(a) to the panel of Medical Visitors unless he is a registered medical practitioner who appears to the Lord Chancellor to have special knowledge and experience of cases of mental disorder;

(b) to the panel of Legal Visitors unless he is a barrister or solicitor of not less than 10 years' standing.

(4) If the Lord Chancellor so determines in the case of any Visitor appointed under this section, he shall be paid out of money provided by Parliament such remuneration and allowances as the Lord Chancellor may, with the concurrence of the Treasury, determine.

## 103 Functions of Visitors

(1) Patients shall be visited by Lord Chancellor's Visitors in such circumstances, and in such manner, as may be prescribed by directions of a standing nature given by the Master of the Court of Protection with the concurrence of the Lord Chancellor.

(2) Where it appears to the judge in the case of any patient that a visit by a Lord Chancellor's Visitor is necessary for the purpose of investigating any particular matter or matters relating to the capacity of the patient to manage and administer his property and affairs, or otherwise relating to the exercise in relation to him of the functions of the judge under this Part of this Act, the judge may order that the patient shall be visited for that purpose.

(3) Every visit falling to be made under subsection (1) or (2) above shall be made by a General Visitor unless, in a case where it appears to the judge that it is in the circumstances essential for the visit to be made by a Visitor with medical or legal qualifications, the judge directs that the visit shall be made by a Medical or a Legal Visitor.

(4) A Visitor making a visit under this section shall make such report on the visit as the judge may direct.

(5) A Visitor making a visit under this section may interview the patient in private.

(6) A Medical Visitor making a visit under this section may carry out in private a medical examination of the patient and may require the production of and inspect any medical records relating to the patient.

(7) The Master of the Court of Protection may visit any patient for the purpose mentioned in subsection (2) above and may interview the patient in private.

(8) A report made by a Visitor under this section, and information contained in such a report, shall not be disclosed except to the judge and any person authorised by the judge to receive the disclosure.

(9) If any person discloses any report or information in contravention of subsection (8) above, he shall be guilty of an offence and liable on summary conviction to imprisonment for a term not exceeding three months or to a fine not exceeding level 3 on the standard scale or both.

(10) In this section references to patients include references to persons alleged to be incapable, by reason of mental disorder, of managing and administering their property and affairs.

## 104 General powers of the judge with respect to proceedings

(1) For the purposes of any proceedings before him with respect to persons suffering or alleged to be suffering from mental disorder, the judge shall have the same powers as are vested in the High Court in respect of securing the attendance of witnesses and the production of documents.

(2) Subject to the provisions of this section, any act or omission in the course of such proceedings which, if occurring in the course of proceedings in the High Court would have been a contempt of the Court, shall be punishable by the judge in any manner in which it could have been punished by the High Court.

(3) Subsection (2) above shall not authorise the Master, or any other officer of the Court of Protection to exercise any power of attachment or committal, but the Master or officer may certify any such act or omission to the Lord Chancellor or a nominated judge, and the Lord Chancellor or judge may upon such certification inquire into the alleged act or omission and take any such action in relation to it as he could have taken if the proceedings had been before him.

(4) Subsections (1) to (4) of section 36 of the Supreme Court Act 1981 (which provides a special procedure for the issue of writs of subpoena ad testificandum and duces tecum so as to be enforceable throughout the United Kingdom) shall apply in relation to proceedings under this Part of this Act with the substitution for references to the High Court of references to the judge and for references to such writs of references to such document as may be prescribed by rules under this Part of this Act for issue by the judge for securing the attendance of witnesses or the production of documents,

## 105 Appeals

(1) Subject to and in accordance with rules under this Part of this Act, an appeal shall lie to a nominated judge from any decision of the Master of the Court of Protection or any nominated officer.

(2) The Court of Appeal shall continue to have the same jurisdiction as to appeals from any decision of the Lord Chancellor or from any decision of a nominated judge, whether given in the exercise of his original jurisdiction or on the hearing of an appeal under subsection (1) above, as they had immediately before the coming into operation of Part VIII of the Mental Health Act 1959 as to appeals from orders in lunacy made by the Lord Chancellor or any other person having jurisdiction in lunacy.

## 106 Rules of procedure

(1) Proceedings before the judge with respect to persons suffering or alleged to be suffering from mental disorder (in this section referred to as " proceedings ") shall be conducted in accordance with the provisions of rules made under this Part of this Act.

(2) Rules under this Part of this Act may make provision as to—
- (a) the carrying out of preliminary or incidental inquiries;
- (b) the persons by whom and manner in which proceedings may be instituted and carried on;
- (c) the persons who are to be entitled to be notified of, to attend, or to take part in proceedings;

(d) the evidence which may be authorised or required to be given in proceedings and the manner (whether on oath or otherwise and whether orally or in writing) in which it is to be given;

(e) the administration of oaths and taking of affidavits for the purposes of proceedings; and

(f) the enforcement of orders made and directions given in proceedings.

(3) Without prejudice to the provisions of section 104(1) above, rules under this Part of this Act may make provision for authorising or requiring the attendance and examination of persons suffering or alleged to be suffering from mental disorder, the furnishing of information and the production of documents.

(4) Rules under this Part of this Act may make provision as to the termination of proceedings, whether on the death or recovery of the person to whom the proceedings relate or otherwise, and for the exercise, pending the termination of the proceedings, of powers exercisable under this Part of this Act in relation to the property or affairs of a patient.

(5) Rules under this Part of this Act made with the consent of the Treasury may—

(a) make provision as to the scale of costs, fees and percentages payable in relation to proceedings, and as to the manner in which and funds out of which such costs, fees and percentages are to be paid;

(b) contain provision for charging any percentage upon the estate of the person to whom the proceedings relate and for the payment of costs, fees and percentages within such time after the death of the person to whom the proceedings relate or the termination of the proceedings as may be provided by the rules; and

(c) provide for the remission of fees and percentages.

(6) A charge upon the estate of a person created by virtue of subsection (5) above shall not cause any interest of that person in any property to fail or determine or to be prevented from recommencing.

(7) Rules under this Part of this Act may authorise the making of orders for the payment of costs to or by persons attending, as well as persons taking part in, proceedings.

## 107 Security and accounts

(1) Rules under this Part of this Act may make provision as to the giving of security by a receiver and as to the enforcement and discharge of the security.

(2) It shall be the duty of a receiver to render accounts in accordance with the requirements of rules under this Part of this Act, as well after his discharge as during his receivership; and rules under this Part of this Act may make provision for the rendering of accounts by persons other than receivers who are ordered, directed or authorised under this Part of this Act to carry out any transaction.

## 108 General provisions as to rules under Part VII

(1) Any power to make rules conferred by this Part of this Act shall be exercisable by the Lord Chancellor.

(2) Rules under this Part of this Act may contain such incidental and supplemental provisions as appear requisite for the purposes of the rules.

### 109 Effect and proof of orders, etc.

(1) Section 204 of the Law of Property Act 1925 (by which orders of the High Court are made conclusive in favour of purchasers) shall apply in relation to orders made and directions and authorities given by the judge as it applies in relation to orders of the High Court.

(2) Office copies of orders made, directions or authorities given or other instruments issued by the judge and sealed with the official seal of the Court of Protection shall be admissible in all legal proceedings as evidence of the originals without any further proof.

### 110 Reciprocal arrangements in relation to Scotland and Northern Ireland as to exercise of powers

(1) This Part of this Act shall apply in relation to the property and affairs in Scotland or Northern Ireland of a patient in relation to whom powers have been exercised under this Part of this Act, or a person as to whom powers are exercisable and have been exercised under section 98 above as it applies in relation to his property and affairs in England and Wales unless a curator bonis, tutor, judicial factor, committee, receiver or guardian has been appointed for him in Scotland or, as the case may be, Northern Ireland.

(2) Where under the law in force in Scotland or Northern Ireland with respect to the property and affairs of persons suffering from mental disorder a curator bonis, tutor, judicial factor, committee, receiver or guardian has been appointed for any person, the provisions of that law shall apply in relation to that person's property and affairs in England and Wales unless he is a patient in relation to whom powers have been exercised under this Part of this Act, or a person as to whom powers are exercisable and have been exercised under section 98 above.

(3) Nothing in this section shall affect any power to execute a will under section 96(1)(e) above or the effect of any will executed in the exercise of such a power.

(4) In this section references to property do not include references to land or interests in land but this subsection shall not prevent the receipt of rent or other income arising from land or interests in land.

### 111 Construction of references in other Acts to judge or authority having jurisdiction under Part VII

(1) The functions expressed to be conferred by any enactment not contained in this Part of this Act on the judge having jurisdiction under this Part of this Act shall be exercisable by the Lord Chancellor or by a nominated judge.

(2) Subject to subsection (3) below, the functions expressed to be conferred by any such enactment on the authority having jurisdiction under this Part of this Act shall, subject to any express provision to the contrary, be exercisable by the Lord Chancellor, a nominated judge, the Master of the Court of Protection or a nominated officer.

(3) The exercise of the functions referred to in subsection (2) above by a nominated officer shall be subject to any directions of the Master and they shall be exercisable so far only as may be provided by the instrument by which the officer is nominated.

(4) Subject to the foregoing provisions of this section—

(a) references in any enactment not contained in this Part of this Act to the judge having jurisdiction under this Part of this Act shall be construed as references to the Lord Chancellor or a nominated judge, and

(b) references in any such enactment to the authority having jurisdiction under this Part of this Act shall be construed as references to the Lord Chancellor, a nominated judge, the Master of the Court of Protection or a nominated officer.

### 112 Interpretation of Part VII

In this Part of this Act, unless the context otherwise requires—

" nominated judge " means a judge nominated in pursuance of subsection (1) of section 93 above ;

" nominated officer" means an officer nominated in pursuance of subsection (4) of that section ;

" patient" has the meaning assigned to it by section 94 above;

" property " includes any thing in action, and any interest in real or personal property ;

" the judge " shall be construed in accordance with section 94 above;

" will " includes a codicil.

### 113 Disapplication of certain enactments in relation to persons within the jurisdiction of thc judgc

The provisions of the Acts described in Schedule 3 to this Act which are specified in the third column of that Schedule, so far as they make special provision for persons suffering from mental disorder, shall not have effect in relation to patients and to persons as to whom powers are exercisable and have been exercised under section 98 above.

## PART VIII

## MISCELLANEOUS FUNCTIONS OF LOCAL AUTHORITIES AND THE SECRETARY OF STATE

*Approved social workers*

### 114 Appointment of approved social workers

(1) A local social services authority shall appoint a sufficient number of approved social workers for the purpose of discharging the functions conferred on them by this Act.

(2) No person shall be appointed by a local social services authority as an approved social worker unless he is approved by the authority as having appropriate competence in dealing with persons who are suffering from mental disorder.

(3) In approving a person for appointment as an approved social worker a local social services authority shall have regard to such matters as the Secretary of State may direct.

### 115 Powers of entry and inspection

An approved social worker of a local social services authority may at all reasonable times after producing, if asked to do so, some duly authenticated document showing that he is such a social worker, enter and inspect any premises (not being a hospital) in the area of that authority in which a mentally disordered patient is living, if he has reasonable cause to believe that the patient is not under proper care.

*Visiting patients*

### 116 Welfare of certain hospital patients

(1) Where a patient to whom this section applies is admitted to a hospital or nursing home in England and Wales (whether for treatment for mental disorder or for any other reason) then, without prejudice to their duties in relation to the patient apart from the provisions of this section, the authority shall arrange for visits to be made to him on behalf of the authority, and shall take such other steps in relation to the patient while in the hospital or nursing home as would be expected to be taken by his parents.

(2) This section applies to—

(a) a child or young person in respect of whom the rights and powers of a parent are vested in a local authority by virtue of—

(i) section 3 of the Child Care Act 1980 (which relates to the assumption by a local authority of parental rights and duties in relation to a child in their care),

(ii) section 10 of that Act (which relates to the powers and duties of local authorities with respect to persons committed to their care under the Children and Young Persons Act 1969), or

(iii) section 17 of the Social Work (Scotland) Act 1968 (which makes corresponding provision for Scotland);

(b) a person who is subject to the guardianship of a local social services authority under the provisions of this Act or the Mental Health (Scotland) Act 1960; or

(c) a person the functions of whose nearest relative under this Act or under the Mental Health (Scotland) Act 1960 are for the time being transferred to a local social services authority.

*After-care*

### 117 After-care

(1) This section applies to persons who are detained under section 3 above, or admitted to a hospital in pursuance of a hospital order made under section 37 above, or transferred to a hospital in pursuance of a transfer direction made under section 47 or 48 above, and then cease to be detained and leave hospital.

(2) It shall be the duty of the District Health Authority and of the local social services authority to provide, in co-operation with relevant voluntary agencies, after-care services for any person to whom this section applies until such time as the District Health Authority and the local social services authority are satisfied that the person concerned is no longer in need of such services.

(3) In this section " the District Health Authority " means the District Health Authority for the district, and " the local social services authority " means the local social services authority for the area in which the person concerned is resident or to which he is sent on discharge by the hospital in which he was detained.

*Functions of the Secretary of State*

## 118 Code of practice

(1) The Secretary of State shall prepare, and from time to time revise, a code of practice—

(a) for the guidance of registered medical practitioners, managers and staff of hospitals and mental nursing homes and approved social workers in relation to the admission of patients to hospitals and mental nursing homes under this Act; and

(b) for the guidance of registered medical practitioners and members of other professions in relation to the medical treatment of patients suffering from mental disorder.

(2) The code shall, in particular, specify forms of medical treatment in addition to any specified by regulations made for the purposes of section 57 above which in the opinion of the Secretary of State give rise to special concern and which should accordingly not be given by a registered medical practitioner unless the patient has consented to the treatment (or to a plan of treatment including that treatment) and a certificate in writing as to the matters mentioned in subsection (2)(a) and (b) of that section has been given by another registered medical practitioner, being a practitioner appointed for the purposes of this section by the Secretary of State.

(3) Before preparing the code or making any alteration in it the Secretary of State shall consult such bodies as appear to him to be concerned.

(4) The Secretary of State shall lay copies of the code and of any alteration in the code before Parliament; and if either House of Parliament passes a resolution requiring the code or any alteration in it to be withdrawn the Secretary of State shall withdraw the code or alteration and, where he withdraws the code, shall prepare a code in substitution for the one which is withdrawn.

(5) No resolution shall be passed by either House of Parliament under subsection (4) above in respect of a code or alteration after the expiration of the period of 40 days beginning with the day on which a copy of the code or alteration was laid before that House ; but for the purposes of this subsection no account shall be taken of any time during which Parliament is dissolved or prorogued or during which both Houses are adjourned for more than four days.

(6) The Secretary of State shall publish the code as for the time being in force.

## 119 Practitioners approved for purposes of Part IV and s. 118

(1) The Secretary of State may make such provision as he may with the approval of the Treasury determine for the payment of remuneration, allowances, pensions or gratuities to or in respect of registered medical practitioners appointed by him for the purposes of Part IV of this Act and section 118 above and to or in respect of other persons appointed for the purposes of section 57(2)(a) above.

(2) A registered medical practitioner or other person appointed by the Secretary of State for the purposes of the provisions mentioned in subsection (1) above may, for the purpose of exercising his functions under those provisions, at any reasonable time—

(a) visit and interview and, in the case of a registered medical practitioner, examine in private any patient detained in a mental nursing home ; and

(b) require the production of and inspect any records relating to the treatment of the patient in that home.

## 120 General protection of detained patients

(1) The Secretary of State shall keep under review the exercise of the powers and the discharge of the duties conferred or imposed by this Act so far as relating to the detention of patients or to patients liable to be detained under this Act and shall make arrangements for persons authorised by him in that behalf—

(a) to visit and interview in private patients detained under this Act in hospitals and mental nursing homes; and

(b) to investigate—

(i) any complaint made by a person in respect of a matter that occurred while he was detained under this Act in a hospital or mental nursing home and which he considers has not been satisfactorily dealt with by the managers of that hospital or mental nursing home; and

(ii) any other complaint as to the exercise of the powers or the discharge of the duties conferred or imposed by this Act in respect of a person who is or has been so detained.

(2) The arrangements made under this section in respect of the investigation of complaints may exclude matters from investigation in specified circumstances and shall not require any person exercising functions under the arrangements to undertake or continue with any investigation where he does not consider it appropriate to do so.

(3) Where any such complaint as is mentioned in subsection (1)(b)(ii) above is made by a Member of Parliament and investigated under the arrangements made under this section the results of the investigation shall be reported to him.

(4) For the purpose of any such review as is mentioned in subsection (1) above or of carrying out his functions under arrangements made under this section any person authorised in that behalf by the Secretary of State may at any reasonable time—

(a) visit and interview and, if he is a registered medical practitioner, examine in private any patient in a mental nursing home; and

(b) require the production of and inspect any records relating to the detention or treatment of any person who is or has been detained in a mental nursing home.

(5) The matters in respect of which regulations may be made under section 6 of the Nursing Homes Act 1975 shall include the keeping of records relating to the detention and treatment of persons detained under this Act in a mental nursing home.

(6) The Secretary of State may make such provision as he may with the approval of the Treasury determine for the payment of remuneration, allowances, pensions or gratuities to or in respect of persons exercising functions in relation to any such review as is mentioned in subsection (1) above or functions under arrangements made under this section.

(7) The powers and duties referred to in subsection (1) above do not include any power or duty conferred or imposed by Part VII of this Act

## 121 Mental Health Act Commission

(1) Without prejudice to section 126(3) of the National Health Service Act 1977 (power to vary or revoke orders or directions) there shall continue to be a special health authority known as the Mental Health Act Commission established under section 11 of that Act.

(2) Without prejudice to the generality of his powers under section 13 of that Act, the Secretary of State shall direct the Commission to perform on his behalf—

- (a) the function of appointing registered medical practitioners for the purposes of Part IV of this Act and section 118 above and of appointing other persons for the purposes of section 57(2)(a) above; and
- (b) the functions of the Secretary of State under sections 61 and 120(1) and (4) above.

(3) The registered medical practitioners and other persons appointed for the purposes mentioned in subsection (2)(a) above may include members of the Commission.

(4) The Secretary of State may, at the request of or after consultation with the Commission and after consulting such other bodies as appear to him to be concerned, direct the Commission to keep under review the care and treatment, or any aspect of the care and treatment, in hospitals and mental nursing homes of patients who are not liable to be detained under this Act.

(5) For the purpose of any such review as is mentioned in subsection (4) above any person authorised in that behalf by the Commission may at any reasonable time

- (a) visit and interview and, if he is a registered medical practitioner, examine in private any patient in a mental nursing home; and
- (b) require the production of and inspect any records relating to the treatment of any person who is or has been a patient in a mental nursing home.

(6) The Secretary of State may make such provision as he may with the approval of the Treasury determine for the payment of remuneration, allowances, pensions or gratuities to or in respect of persons exercising functions in relation to any such review as is mentioned in subsection (4) above.

(7) The Commission shall review any decision to withhold a postal packet (or anything contained in it) under subsection (1)(b) or (2) of section 134 below if an application in that behalf is made—

- (a) in a case under subsection (1)(b), by the patient; or
- (b) in a case under subsection (2), either by the patient or by the person by whom the postal packet was sent;

and any such application shall be made within six months of the receipt by die applicant of the notice referred to in subsection (6) of that section.

(8) On an application under subsection (7) above the Commission may direct that the postal packet which is the subject of the application (or anything contained in it) shall not be withheld and the managers in question shall comply with any such direction.

(9) The Secretary of State may by regulations make provision with respect to the making and determination of applications under subsection (7) above, including provision for

the production to the Commission of any postal packet which is the subject of such an application.

(10) The Commission shall in the second year after its establishment and subsequently in every second year publish a report on its activities; and copies of every such report shall be sent by the Commission to the Secretary of State who shall lay a copy before each House of Parliament.

(11) Paragraph 9 of Schedule 5 to the said Act of 1977 (pay and allowances for chairmen and members of health authorities) shall have effect in relation to the Mental Health Act Commission as if references in sub-paragraphs (1) and (2) to the chairman included references to any member and as if sub-paragraphs (4) and (5) were omitted.

## 122 Provision of pocket money for in-patients in hospital

(1) The Secretary of State may pay to persons who are receiving treatment as in-patients (whether liable to be detained or not) in special hospitals or other hospitals, being hospitals wholly or mainly used for the treatment of persons suffering from mental disorder, such amounts as he thinks fit in respect of their occasional personal expenses where it appears to him that they would otherwise be without resources to meet those expenses.

(2) For the purposes of the National Health Service Act 1977, the making of payments under this section to persons for whom hospital services are provided under that Act shall be treated as included among those services.

## 123 Transfers to and from special hospitals

(1) Without prejudice to any other provisions of this Act with respect to the transfer of patients, any patient who is for the time being liable to be detained in a special hospital under this Act (other than under section 35, 36 or 38 above) may, upon the directions of the Secretary of State, at any time be removed into any other special hospital.

(2) Without prejudice to any such provision, the Secretary of State may give directions for the transfer of any patient who is for the time being liable to be so detained into a hospital which is not a special hospital.

(3) Subsections (2) and (4) of section 19 above shall apply in relation to the transfer or removal of a patient under this section as they apply in relation to the transfer or removal of a patient from one hospital to another under that section.

## 124 Default powers of Secretary of State

(1) Where the Secretary of State is of the opinion, on complaint or otherwise, that a local social services authority have failed to carry out functions conferred or imposed on the authority by or under this Act or have in carrying out those functions failed to comply with any regulations relating to those functions, he may after such inquiry as he thinks fit make an order declaring the authority to be in default.

(2) Subsections (3) to (5) of section 85 of the National Health Service Act 1977 (which relates to orders declaring, among others, a local social services authority to be in default under that Act) shall apply in relation to an order under this section as they apply in relation to an order under that section.

## 125 Inquiries

(1) The Secretary of State may cause an inquiry to be held in any case where he thinks it advisable to do so in connection with any matter arising under this Act.

(2) Subsections (2) to (5) of section 250 of the Local Government Act 1972 shall apply to any inquiry held under this Act, except that no local authority shall be ordered to pay costs under subsection (4) of that section in the case of any inquiry unless the authority is a party to the inquiry.

# PART IX

OFFENCES

## 126 Forgery, false statements, etc.

(1) Any person who without lawful authority or excuse has in his custody or under his control any document to which this subsection applies, which is, and which he knows or believes to be, false within the meaning of Part I of the Forgery and Counterfeiting Act 1981, shall be guilty of an offence.

(2) Any person who without lawful authority or excuse makes or has in his custody or under his control, any document so closely resembling a document to which subsection (1) above applies as to be calculated to deceive shall be guilty of an offence.

(3) The documents to which subsection (1) above applies are any documents purporting to be—

(a) an application under Part II of this Act;

(b) a medical recommendation or report under this Act; and

(c) any other document required or authorised to be made for any of the purposes of this Act.

(4) Any person who—

(a) wilfully makes a false entry or statement in any application, recommendation, report, record or other document required or authorised to be made for any of the purposes of this Act; or

(b) with intent to deceive, makes use of any such entry or statement which he knows to be false,

shall be guilty of an offence.

(5) Any person guilty of an offence under this section shall be liable—

(a) on summary conviction, to imprisonment for a term not exceeding six months or to a fine not exceeding the statutory maximum, or to both ;

(b) on conviction on indictment, to imprisonment for a term not exceeding two years or to a fine of any amount, or to both.

## 127 Ill-treatment of patients

(1) It shall be an offence for any person who is an officer on the staff of or otherwise employed in, or who is one of the managers of, a hospital or mental nursing home—

(a) to ill-treat or wilfully to neglect a patient for the time being receiving treatment for mental disorder as an in-patient in that hospital or home; or

(b) to ill-treat or wilfully to neglect, on the premises of which the hospital or home forms part, a patient for the time being receiving such treatment there as an out-patient.

(2) It shall be an offence for any individual to ill-treat or wilfully to neglect a mentally disordered patient who is for the time being subject to his guardianship under this Act or otherwise in his custody or care (whether by virtue of any legal or moral obligation or otherwise).

(3) Any person guilty of an offence under this section shall be liable—

(a) on summary conviction, to imprisonment for a term not exceeding six months or to a fine not exceeding the statutory maximum, or to both;

(b) on conviction on indictment, to imprisonment for a term not exceeding two years or to a fine of any amount, or to both.

(4) No proceedings shall be instituted for an offence under this section except by or with the consent of the Director of Public Prosecutions.

### 128 Assisting patients to absent themselves without leave, etc.

(1) Where any person induces or knowingly assists another person who is liable to be detained in a hospital within the meaning of Part II of this Act or is subject to guardianship under this Act to absent himself without leave he shall be guilty of an offence.

(2) Where any person induces or knowingly assists another person who is in legal custody by virtue of section 137 below to escape from such custody he shall be guilty of an offence.

(3) Where any person knowingly harbours a patient who is absent without leave or is otherwise at large and liable to be retaken under this Act or gives him any assistance with intent to prevent, hinder or interfere with his being taken into custody or returned to the hospital or other place where he ought to be he shall be guilty of an offence.

(4) Any person guilty of an offence under this section shall be liable—

(a) on summary conviction, to imprisonment for a term not exceeding six months or to a fine not exceeding the statutory maximum, or to both ;

(b) on conviction on indictment, to imprisonment for a term not exceeding two years or to a fine of any amount, or to both.

### 129 Obstruction

(1) Any person who without reasonable cause—

(a) refuses to allow the inspection of any premises ; or

(b) refuses to allow the visiting, interviewing or examination of any person by a person authorised in that behalf by or under this Act; or

(c) refuses to produce for the inspection of any person so authorised any document or record the production of which is duly required by him ; or

(d) otherwise obstructs any such person in the exercise of his functions,

shall be guilty of an offence.

(2) Without prejudice to the generality of subsection (1) above, any person who insists on being present when required to withdraw by a person authorised by or under this Act to interview or examine a person in private shall be guilty of an offence.

(3) Any person guilty of an offence under this section shall be liable on summary conviction to imprisonment for a term not exceeding three months or to a fine not exceeding level 4 on the standard scale or to both.

### 130 Prosecutions by local authorities

A local social services authority may institute proceedings for any offence under this Part of this Act, but without prejudice to any provision of this Part of this Act requiring the consent of the Director of Public Prosecutions for the institution of such proceedings.

## PART X

## MISCELLANEOUS AND SUPPLEMENTARY

*Miscellaneous provisions*

### 131 Informal admission of patients

(1) Nothing in this Act shall be construed as preventing a patient who requires treatment for mental disorder from being admitted to any hospital or mental nursing home in pursuance of arrangements made in that behalf and without any application, order or direction rendering him liable to be detained under this Act, or from remaining in any hospital or mental nursing home in pursuance of such arrangements after he has ceased to be so liable to be detained.

(2) In the case of a minor who has attained the age of 16 years and is capable of expressing his own wishes, any such arrangements as are mentioned in subsection (1) above may be made, carried out and determined notwithstanding any right of custody or control vested by law in his parent or guardian.

### 132 Duty of managers of hospitals to give information to detained patients

(1) The managers of a hospital or mental nursing home in which a patient is detained under this Act shall take such steps as are practicable to ensure that the patient understands—

(a) under which of the provisions of this Act he is for the time being detained and the effect of that provision; and

(b) what rights of applying to a Mental Health Review Tribunal are available to him in respect of his detention under that provision; and those steps shall be taken as soon as practicable after the commencement of the patient's detention under the provision in question.

(2) The managers of a hospital or mental nursing home in which a patient is detained as aforesaid shall also take such steps as are practicable to ensure that the patient understands the effect, so far as relevant in his case, of sections 23, 25, 56 to 64, 66(1)(g), 118 and 120 above and section 134 below; and those steps shall be taken as soon

as practicable after the commencement of the patient's detention in the hospital or nursing home.

(3) The steps to be taken under subsections (1) and (2) above shall include giving the requisite information both orally and in writing.

(4) The managers of a hospital or mental nursing home in which a patient is detained as aforesaid shall, except where the patient otherwise requests, take such steps as are practicable to furnish the person (if any) appearing to them to be his nearest relative with a copy of any information given to him in writing under subsections (1) and (2) above; and those steps shall be taken when the information is given to the patient or within a reasonable time thereafter.

## 133 Duty of managers of hospitals to inform nearest relatives of discharge

(1) Where a patient liable to be detained under this Act in a hospital or mental nursing home is to be discharged otherwise than by virtue of an order for discharge made by his nearest relative, the managers of the hospital or mental nursing home shall, subject to subsection (2) below, take such steps as are practicable to inform the person (if any) appearing to them to be the nearest relative of the patient; and that information shall, if practicable, be given at least seven days before the date of discharge.

(2) Subsection (1) above shall not apply if the patient or his nearest relative has requested that information about the patient's discharge should not be given under this section.

## 134 Correspondence of patients

(1) A postal packet addressed to any person by a patient detained in a hospital under this Act and delivered by the patient for dispatch may be withheld from the Post Office—

(a) if that person has requested that communications addressed to him by the patient should be withheld ; or

(b) subject to subsection (3) below, if the hospital is a special hospital and the managers of the hospital consider that the postal packet is likely—

(i) to cause distress to the person to whom it is addressed or to any other person (not being a person on the staff of the hospital); or

(ii) to cause danger to any person;

and any request for the purposes of paragraph (a) above shall be made by a notice in writing given to the managers of the hospital, the registered medical practitioner in charge of the treatment of the patient or the Secretary of State.

(2) Subject to subsection (3) below, a postal packet addressed to a patient detained in a special hospital under this Act may be withheld from the patient if, in the opinion of the managers of the hospital, it is necessary to do so in the interests of the safety of the patient or for the protection of other persons.

(3) Subsections (1)(b) and (2) above do not apply to any postal packet addressed by a patient to, or sent to a patient by or on behalf of—

(a) any Minister of the Crown or Member of either House of Parliament;

(b) the Master or any other officer of the Court of Protection or any of the Lord Chancellor's Visitors ;

(c) the Parliamentary Commissioner for Administration, the Health Service Commissioner for England, the Health Service Commissioner for Wales or a

Local Commissioner within the meaning of Part III of the Local Government Act 1974;

(d) a Mental Health Review Tribunal;

(e) a health authority within the meaning of the National Health Service Act 1977, a local social services authority, a Community Health Council or a probation and after-care committee appointed under paragraph 2 of Schedule 3 to the Powers of Criminal Courts Act 1973;

(f) the managers of the hospital in which the patient is detained;

(g) any legally qualified person instructed by the patient to act as his legal adviser; or

(h) the European Commission of Human Rights or the European Court of Human Rights.

(4) The managers of a hospital may inspect and open any postal packet for the purposes of determining—

(a) whether it is one to which subsection (1) or (2) applies, and

(b) in the case of a postal packet to which subsection (1) or (2) above applies, whether or not it should be withheld under that subsection;

and the power to withhold a postal packet under either of those subsections includes power to withhold anything contained in it.

(5) Where a postal packet or anything contained in it is withheld under subsection (1) or (2) above the managers of the hospital shall record that fact in writing.

(6) Where a postal packet or anything contained in it is withheld under subsection (1)(b) or (2) above the managers of the hospital shall within seven days give notice of that fact to the patient and, in the case of a packet withheld under subsection (2) above, to the person (if known) by whom the postal packet was sent; and any such notice shall be given in writing and shall contain a statement of the effect of section 121(7) and (8) above.

(7) The functions of the managers of a hospital under this section shall be discharged on their behalf by a person on the staff of the hospital appointed by them for that purpose and different persons may be appointed to discharge different functions.

(8) The Secretary of State may make regulations with respect to the exercise of the powers conferred by this section.

(9) In this section " hospital" has the same meaning as in Part II of this Act, " postal packet" has the same meaning as in the Post Office Act 1953 and the provisions of this section shall have effect notwithstanding anything in section 56 of that Act.

### 135 Warrant to search for and remove patients

(1) If it appears to a justice of the peace, on information on oath laid by an approved social worker, that there is reasonable cause to suspect that a person believed to be suffering from mental disorder—

(a) has been, or is being, ill-treated, neglected or kept otherwise than under proper control, in any place within the jurisdiction of the justice, or

(b) being unable to care for himself, is living alone in any such place,

the justice may issue a warrant authorising any constable named in the warrant to enter, if need be by force, any premises specified in the warrant in which that person is believed to be, and, if thought fit, to remove him to a place of safety with a view to the making of an application in respect of him under Part II of this Act, or of other arrangements for his treatment or care.

(2) If it appears to a justice of the peace, on information on oath laid by any constable or other person who is authorised by or under this Act or under section 83 of the Mental Health (Scotland) Act 1960 to take a patient to any place, or to take into custody or retake a patient who is liable under this Act or under the said section 83 to be so taken or retaken—

(a) that there is reasonable cause to believe that the patient is to be found on premises within the jurisdiction of the justice; and

(b) that admission to the premises has been refused or that a refusal of such admission is apprehended,

the justice may issue a warrant authorising any constable named in the warrant to enter the premises, if need be by force, and remove the patient.

(3) A patient who is removed to a place of safety in the execution of a warrant issued under this section may be detained there for a period not exceeding 72 hours.

(4) In the execution of a warrant issued under subsection (1) above, the constable to whom it is addressed shall be accompanied by an approved social worker and by a registered medical practitioner, and in the execution of a warrant issued under subsection (2) above the constable to whom it is addressed may be accompanied—

(a) by a registered medical practitioner;

(b) by any person authorised by or under this Act or under section 83 of the Mental Health (Scotland) Act 1960 to take or retake the patient.

(5) It shall not be necessary in any information or warrant under subsection (1) above to name the patient concerned.

(6) In this section " place of safety" means residential accommodation provided by a local social services authority under Part III of the National Assistance Act 1948 or under paragraph 2 of Schedule 8 to the National Health Service Act 1977, a hospital as defined by this Act, a police station, a mental nursing home or residential home for mentally disordered persons or any other suitable place the occupier of which is willing temporarily to receive the patient.

### 136 Mentally disordered persons found in public places

(1) If a constable finds in a place to which the public have access a person who appears to him to be suffering from mental disorder and to be in immediate need of care or control, the constable may, if he thinks it necessary to do so in the interests of that person or for the protection of other persons, remove that person to a place of safety within the meaning of section 135 above.

(2) A person removed to a place of safety under this section may be detained there for a period not exceeding 72 hours for the purpose of enabling him to be examined by a registered medical practitioner and to be interviewed by an approved social worker and of making any necessary arrangements for his treatment or care.

### 137 Provisions as to custody, conveyance and detention

(1) Any person required or authorised by or by virtue of this Act to be conveyed to any place or to be kept in custody or detained in a place of safety or at any place to which

he is taken under section 42(6) above shall, while being so conveyed, detained or kept, as the case may be, be deemed to be in legal custody.

(2) A constable or any other person required or authorised by or by virtue of this Act to take any person into custody, or to convey or detain any person shall, for the purposes of taking him into custody or conveying or detaining him, have all the powers, authorities, protection and privileges which a constable has within the area for which he acts as constable.

(3) In this section " convey " includes any other expression denoting removal from one place to another.

### 138 Retaking of patients escaping from custody

(1) If any person who is in legal custody by virtue of section 137 above escapes, he may, subject to the provisions of this section, be retaken—

(a) in any case, by the person who had his custody immediately before the escape, or by any constable or approved social worker;

(b) if at the time of the escape he, was liable to be detained in a hospital within the meaning of Part II of this Act, or subject to guardianship under this Act, by any other person who could take him into custody under section 18 above if he had absented himself without leave.

(2) A person to whom paragraph (b) of subsection (1) above applies shall not be retaken under this section after the expiration of the period within which he could be retaken under section 18 above if he had absented himself without leave on the day of the escape unless he is subject to a restriction order under Part III of this Act or an order or direction having the same effect as such an order; and subsection (4) of the said section 18 shall apply with the necessary modifications accordingly.

(3) A person who escapes while being taken to or detained in a place of safety under section 135 or 136 above shall not be retaken under this section after the expiration of the period of 72 hours beginning with the time when he escapes or the period during which he is liable to be so detained, whichever expires first.

(4) This section, so far as it relates to the escape of a person liable to be detained in a hospital within the meaning of Part II of this Act, shall apply in relation to a person who escapes—

(a) while being taken to or from such a hospital in pursuance of regulations under section 19 above, or of any order, direction or authorisation under Part III or VI of this Act (other than under section 35, 36, 38, 53, 83 or 85) or under section 123 above; or

(b) while being taken to or detained in a place of safety in pursuance of an order under Part III of this Act (other than under section 35, 36 or 38 above) pending his admission to such a hospital,

as if he were liable to be detained in that hospital and, if he had not previously been received in that hospital, as if he had been so received.

(5) In computing for the purposes of the power to give directions under section 37(4) above and for the purposes of sections 37(5) and 40(1) above the period of 28 days mentioned in those sections, no account shall be taken of any time during which the patient is at large and liable to be retaken by virtue of this section.

(6) Section 21 above shall, with any necessary modifications, apply in relation to a patient who is at large and liable to be retaken by virtue of this section as it applies in relation to a patient who is absent without leave and references in that section to section 18 above shall be construed accordingly.

### 139 Protection for acts done in pursuance of this Act

(1) No person shall be liable, whether on the ground of want of jurisdiction or on any other ground, to any civil or criminal proceedings to which he would have been liable apart from this section in respect of any act purporting to be done in pursuance of this Act or any regulations or rules made under this Act, or in, or in pursuance of anything done in, the discharge of functions conferred by any other enactment on the authority having jurisdiction under Part VII of this Act, unless the act was done in bad faith or without reasonable care.

(2) No civil proceedings shall be brought against any person in any court in respect of any such act without the leave of the High Court; and no criminal proceedings shall be brought against any person in any court in respect of any such act except by or with the consent of the Director of Public Prosecutions.

(3) This section does not apply to proceedings for an offence under this Act, being proceedings which, under any other provision of this Act, can be instituted only by or with the consent of the Director of Public Prosecutions.

(4) This section does not apply to proceedings against the Secretary of State or against a health authority within the meaning of the National Health Service Act 1977.

(5) In relation to Northern Ireland the reference in this section to the Director of Public Prosecutions shall be construed as a reference to the Director of Public Prosecutions for Northern Ireland.

### 140 Notification of hospitals having arrangements for reception of urgent cases

It shall be the duty of every Regional Health Authority and in Wales every District Health Authority to give notice to every local social services authority for an area wholly or partly comprised within the region or district, as the case may be, of the Authority specifying the hospital or hospitals administered by the Authority in which arrangements are from time to time in force for the reception, in case of special urgency, of patients requiring treatment for mental disorder.

### 141 Members of Parliament suffering from mental illness

(1) Where a member of the House of Commons is authorised to be detained on the ground (however formulated) that he is suffering from mental illness, it shall be the duty of the court, authority or person on whose order or application, and of any registered medical practitioner upon whose recommendation or certificate, the detention was authorised, and of the person in charge of the hospital or other place in which the member is authorised to be detained, to notify the Speaker of the House of Commons that the detention has been authorised.

(2) Where the Speaker receives a notification under subsection (1) above, or is notified by two members of the House of Commons that they are credibly informed that such an authorisation has been given, the Speaker shall cause the member to whom the

notification relates to be visited and examined by two registered medical practitioners appointed in accordance with subsection (3) below.

(3) The registered medical practitioners to be appointed for the purposes of subsection (2) above shall be appointed by the President of the Royal College of Psychiatrists and shall be practitioners appearing to the President to have special experience in the diagnosis or treatment of mental disorders.

(4) The registered medical practitioners appointed in accordance with subsection (3) above shall report to the Speaker whether the member is suffering from mental illness and is authorised to be detained as such.

(5) If the report is to the effect that the member is suffering from mental illness and authorised to be detained as aforesaid, the Speaker shall at the expiration of six months from the date of the report, if the House is then sitting, and otherwise as soon as may be after the House next sits, again cause the member to be visited and examined by two such registered medical practitioners as aforesaid, and the registered medical practitioners shall report as aforesaid.

(6) If the second report is that the member is suffering from mental illness and authorised to be detained as mentioned in subsection (4) above, the Speaker shall forthwith lay both reports before the House of Commons, and thereupon the seat of the member shall become vacant.

(7) Any sums required for the payment of fees and expenses to registered medical practitioners acting in relation to a member of the House of Commons under this section shall be defrayed out of moneys provided by Parliament.

**142 Pay, pensions, etc., of mentally disordered persons**

(1) Where a periodic payment falls to be made to any person by way of pay or pension or otherwise in connection with the service or employment of that or any other person, and the payment falls to be made directly out of moneys provided by Parliament or the Consolidated Fund, or other moneys administered by or under the control or supervision of a government department, the authority by whom the sum in question is payable, if satisfied after considering medical evidence that the person to whom it is payable (referred to in this section as " the patient") is incapable by reason of mental disorder of managing and administering his property and affairs, may, instead of paying the sum to the patient, apply it in accordance with subsection (2) below.

(2) The authority may pay the sum or such part of it as they think fit to the institution or person having the care of the patient, to be applied for his benefit and may pay the remainder (if any) or such part of the remainder as they think fit—

(a) to or for the benefit of persons who appear to the authority to be members of the patient's family or other persons for whom the patient might be expected to provide if he were not mentally disordered, or

(b) in reimbursement, with or without interest, of money applied by any person either in payment of the patient's debts (whether legally enforceable or not) or for the maintenance or other benefit of the patient or such persons as are mentioned in paragraph (a) above.

(3) In this section " government department" does not include a Northern Ireland department.

### *Supplemental*

## 143 General provisions as to regulations, orders and rules

(1) Any power of the Secretary of State or the Lord Chancellor to make regulations, orders or rules under this Act shall be exercisable by statutory instrument.

(2) Any Order in Council under this Act and any statutory instrument containing regulations or rules made under this Act shall be subject to annulment in pursuance of a resolution of either House of Parliament.

(3) No order shall be made under section 68(4) or 71(3) above unless a draft of it has been approved by a resolution of each House of Parliament.

## 144 Power to amend local Acts

Her Majesty may by Order in Council repeal or amend any local enactment so far as appears to Her Majesty to be necessary in consequence of this Act.

## 145 Interpretation

(1) In this Act, unless the context otherwise requires—

" absent without leave " has the meaning given to it by section 18 above and related expressions shall be construed accordingly;

" application for admission for assessment" has the meaning given in section 2 above ;

" application for admission for treatment" has the meaning given in section 3 above ;

" approved social worker " means an officer of a local social services authority appointed to act as an approved social worker for the purposes of this Act;

" hospital" means—

(a) any health service hospital within the meaning of the National Health Service Act 1977 ; and

(b) any accommodation provided by a local authority and used as a hospital by or on behalf of the Secretary of State under that Act;

and " hospital within the meaning of Part II of this Act" has the meaning given in section 34 above ;

" hospital order " and " guardianship order " have the meanings respectively given in section 37 above ;

" interim hospital order " has the meaning given in section 38 above;

" local social services authority " means a council which is a local authority for the purpose of the Local Authority Social Services Act 1970 ;

" the managers " means—

(a) in relation to a hospital vested in the Secretary of State for the purposes of his functions under the National Health Service Act 1977, and in relation to any accommodation provided by a local authority and used as a hospital by or on behalf of the Secretary of State under that Act, the District Health Authority or special health authority responsible for the administration of the hospital;

(b) in relation to a special hospital, the Secretary of State;

(c) in relation to a mental nursing home registered in pursuance of the Nursing Homes Act 1975, the person or persons registered in respect of the home;

and in this definition " hospital" means a hospital within the meaning of Part II of this Act;

"medical treatment" includes nursing, and also includes care, habilitation and rehabilitation under medical supervision;

" mental disorder ", " severe mental impairment", " mental impairment" and "psychopathic disorder" have the meanings given in section 1 above ;

" mental nursing home " has the same meaning as in the Nursing Homes Act 1975 ;

" nearest relative ", in relation to a patient, has the meaning given in Part II of this Act;

" patient" (except in Part VII of this Act) means a person suffering or appearing to be suffering from mental disorder;

" restriction direction " has the meaning given to it by section 49 above;

" restriction order" has the meaning given to it by section 41 above;

" special hospital " has the same meaning as in the National Health Service Act 1977 ;

" standard scale " has the meaning given in section 75 of the Criminal Justice Act 1982 ;

" transfer direction " has the meaning given to it by section 47 above.

(2) " Statutory maximum " has the meaning given in section 74 of the Criminal Justice Act 1982 and for the purposes of section 128(4)(a) above—

(a) subsection (1) of section 74 shall have effect as if after the words " England and Wales " there were inserted the words " or Northern Ireland " ; and

(b) section 32 of the Magistrates' Courts Act 1980 shall extend to Northern Ireland.

(3) In relation to a person who is liable to be detained or subject to guardianship by virtue of an order or direction under Part III of this Act (other than under section 35, 36 or 38), any reference in this Act to any enactment contained in Part II of this Act or in section 66 or 67 above shall be construed as a reference to that enactment as it applies to that person by virtue of Part III of this Act.

## 146 Application to Scotland

Sections 42(6), 80, 88 (and so far as applied by that section sections 18, 22 and 138), 104(4), 110 (and so much of Part VII of this Act as is applied in relation to Scotland by that section), 116, 122, 128 (except so far as it relates to patients subject to guardianship), 137, 139(1), 141, 142, 143 (so far as applicable to any Order in Council extending to Scotland) and 144 above shall extend to Scotland together with any amendment or repeal by this Act of or any provision of Schedule 5 to this Act relating to any enactment which so extends; but, except as aforesaid and except so far as it relates to the interpretation or commencement of the said provisions, this Act shall not extend to Scotland.

### 147 Application to Northern Ireland

Sections 81, 82, 86, 87, 88 (and so far as applied by that section sections 18, 22 and 138), 104(4), 110 (and so much of Part VII as is applied in relation to Northern Ireland by that section), section 128 (except so far as it relates to patients subject to guardianship), 137, 139, 141, 142, 143 (so far as applicable to any Order in Council extending to Northern Ireland) and 144 above shall extend to Northern Ireland together with any amendment or repeal by this Act of or any provision of Schedule 5 to this Act relating to any enactment which so extends; but except as aforesaid and except so far as it relates to the interpretation or commencement of the said provisions, this Act shall not extend to Northern Ireland.

### 148 Consequential and transitional provisions and repeals

(1) Schedule 4 (consequential amendments) and Schedule 5 (transitional and saving provisions) to this Act shall have effect but without prejudice to the operation of sections 15 to 17 of the Interpretation Act 1978 (which relate to the effect of repeals).

(2) Where any amendment in Schedule 4 to this Act affects an enactment amended by the Mental Health (Amendment) Act 1982 the amendment in Schedule 4 shall come into force immediately after the provision of the Act of 1982 amending that enactment.

(3) The enactments specified in Schedule 6 to this Act are hereby repealed to the extent mentioned in the third column of that Schedule.

### 149 Short title, commencement and application to Scilly Isles

(1) This Act may be cited as the Mental Health Act 1983.

(2) Subject to subsection (3) below and Schedule 5 to this Act. this Act shall come into force on 30th September 1983.

(3) Sections 35, 36, 38 and 40(3) above shall come into force on such day (not being earlier than the said 30th September) as may be appointed by the Secretary of State and a different day may be appointed for each of those sections or for different purposes of any of those sections.

(4) Section 130(4) of the National Health Service Act 1977 (which provides for the extension of that Act to the Isles of Scilly) shall have effect as if the references to that Act included references to this Act.

# SCHEDULES

## SCHEDULE 1

Section 40(4), 41(3) and (5), and 55(4).

APPLICATION OF CERTAIN PROVISIONS TO PATIENTS SUBJECT TO HOSPITAL AND GUARDIANSHIP ORDERS

### PART I

PATIENTS NOT SUBJECT TO SPECIAL RESTRICTIONS

1 Sections 9, 10, 17, 21, 24(3) and (4), 26 to 28, 31, 32, 34, 67 and 76 shall apply in relation to the patient without modification.

2 Sections 16, 18, 19, 20, 22, 23 and 66 shall apply in relation to the patient with the modifications specified in paragraphs 3 to 9 below.

3 In section 16(1) for references to an application for admission or a guardianship application there shall be substituted references to the order or direction under Part III of this Act by virtue of which the patient is liable to be detained or subject to guardianship.

4 In section 18 subsection (5) shall be omitted.

5 In section 19(2) for the words from " as follows " to the end of the subsection there shall be substituted the words " as if the order or direction under Part III of this Act by virtue of which he was liable to be detained or subject to guardianship before being transferred were an order or direction for his admission or removal to the hospital to which he is transferred, or placing him under the guardianship of the authority or person into whose guardianship he is transferred, as the case may be " .

6 In section 20—

(a) in subsection (1) for the words from " day on which he was " to " as the case may be " there shall be substituted the words " date of the relevant order or direction under Part III of this Act " ; and

(b) in subsection (9) for the words " the application for admission for treatment or, as the case may be, in the guardianship application, that application " there shall be substituted the words " the relevant order or direction under Part III of this Act, that order or direction " .

7 In section 22 for references to an application for admission or a guardianship application there shall be substituted references to the order or direction under Part III of this Act by virtue of which the patient is liable to be detained or subject to guardianship.

8 In section 23(2)—

(a) in paragraph (a) the words " for assessment or" shall be omitted; and

(b) in paragraphs (a) and (b) the references to the nearest relative shall be omitted.

9 In section 66—

(a) in subsection (1), paragraphs (a), (b), (c), (g) and (h), the words in parenthesis in paragraph (i) and paragraph (ii) shall be omitted; and

(b) in subsection (2), paragraphs (a), (b) (c) and (g) shall be omitted and in paragraph (d) for the words " cases mentioned in paragraphs (d) and (g) " there shall be substituted the words " case mentioned in paragraph (d) " .

## PART II

### Patients Subject to Special Restrictions

1 Sections 24(3) and (4), 32 and 76 shall apply in relation to the patient without modification.

2 Sections 17 to 19, 22, 23 and 34 shall apply in relation to the patient with the modifications specified in paragraphs 3 to 8 below.

3 In section 17—

(a) in subsection (1) after the word "may" there shall be inserted the words " with the consent of the Secretary of State " ;

(b) in subsection (4) after the words "the responsible medical officer " and after the words " that officer " there shall be inserted the words " or the Secretary of State " ; and

(c) in subsection (5) after the word " recalled " there shall be inserted the words " by the responsible medical officer " ,

and for the words from " he has ceased" to the end of the subsection there shall be substituted the words " the expiration of the period of six months beginning with the first day of his absence on leave " .

4 In section 18 there shall be omitted—

(a) in subsection (1) the words "subject to the provisions of this section " ; and

(b) subsections (3), (4) and (5).

5 In section 19—

(a) in subsection (1) after the word " may " in paragraph (a) there shall be inserted the words " with the consent of lie Secretary of State " , and the words from "or into" to the end of the subsection shall be omitted; and

(b) in subsection (2) for the words from " as follows " to the end of the subsection there shall be substituted the words " as if the order or direction under Part III of this Act by virtue of which he was liable to be detained before being transferred were an order or direction for his admission or removal to the hospital to which he is transferred " .

6 In section 22 subsection (1) and paragraph (a) of subsection (2) shall not apply.

7 In section 23—

(a) in subsection (1) references to guardianship shall be omitted and after the word " made " there shall be inserted the words " with the consent of the Secretary of State and " , and

(b) in subsection (2)—

(i) in paragraph (a) the words " for assessment or" and " or by the nearest relative of the patient" shall be omitted ; and

(ii) paragraph (b) shall be omitted.

8 In section 34, in subsection (1) the definition of " the nominated medical attendant" and subsection (3) shall be omitted.

## SCHEDULE 2

Section 65(2).

### Mental Health Review Tribunals

1 Each of the Mental Health Review Tribunals shall consist of—

(a) a number of persons (referred to in this Schedule as "the legal members ") appointed by the Lord Chancellor and having such legal experience as the Lord Chancellor considers suitable ;

(b) a number of persons (referred to in this Schedule as "the medical members ") being registered medical practitioners appointed by the Lord Chancellor after consultation with the Secretary of State ; and

(c) a number of persons appointed by the Lord Chancellor after consultation with the Secretary of State and having such experience in administration, such knowledge of social services or such other qualifications or experience as the Lord Chancellor considers suitable.

2 The members of Mental Health Review Tribunals shall hold and vacate office under the terms of the instrument under which they are appointed, but may resign office by notice in writing to the Lord Chancellor; and any such member who ceases to hold office shall be eligible for re-appointment

3 One of the legal members of each Mental Health Review Tribunal shall be appointed by the Lord Chancellor as chairman of the Tribunal.

4 Subject to rules made by the Lord Chancellor under section 78(2)(c) above, the members who are to constitute a Mental Health Review Tribunal for the purposes of any proceedings or class or group of proceedings under this Act shall be appointed by the chairman of the tribunal or, if for any reason he is unable to act, by another member of the tribunal appointed for the purpose by the chairman ; and of the members so appointed—

(a) one or more shall be appointed from the legal members ;

(b) one or more shall be appointed from the medical members ; and

(c) one or more shall be appointed from the members who are neither legal nor medical members.

5 A member of a Mental Health Review Tribunal for any area may be appointed under paragraph 4 above as one of the persons to constitute a Mental Health Review Tribunal for any other area for the purposes of any proceedings or class or group of proceedings ; and for the purposes of this Act, a person so appointed shall, in relation to the proceedings for which he was appointed, be deemed to be a member of that other tribunal.

6 Subject to any rules made by the Lord Chancellor under section 78(4)(a) above, where the chairman of the tribunal is included among the persons appointed under paragraph 4 above, he shall be president of the tribunal; and in any other case the president of the tribunal shall be such one of the members so appointed (being one of the legal members) as the chairman may nominate.

# SCHEDULE 3

Section 113.

## ENACTMENTS DISAPPLIED IN RESPECT OF PERSONS WITHIN JURISDICTION UNDER PART VII

| Session and Chapter | Short Title | Enactments |
|---|---|---|
| 13 Geo. 3. c.81. | The Inclosure Act 1773. | Sections 22 and 24. |
| 7 Geo. 4. c. 16. | The Chelsea and Kilmainham Hospitals Act 1826. | Sections 44 to 48. |
| 2 & 3 Will. 4. c. 80. | The Ecclesiastical Corporations Act 1832. | Section 3. |
| 1 & 2 Vict. c. 106. | The Pluralities Act 1838. | Section 127. |
| 4 & 5 Vict. c. 38. | The School Sites Act 1841. | Section 5. |
| 5 & 6 Vict. c. 26. | The Ecclesiastical Houses of Residence Act 1842. | Section 12. |
| 5 & 6 Vict. c. 108. | The Ecclesiastical Leasing Act 1842. | Section 24. |
| 8 & 9 Vict. c. 16. | The Companies Clauses Consolidation Act 1845. | Section 79. |
| 8 & 9 Vict. c. 18. | The Lands Clauses Consolidation Act 1845. | Section 9. |
| 8 & 9 Vict. c. 118. | The Inclosure Act 1845. | Sections 20, 133, 134 and 137. |
| 9 & 10 Vict. c. 73. | The Tithe Act 1846. | Sections 5, 9 and 10. |
| 17 & 18 Vict. c. 112. | The Literary and Scientific Institutions Act 1854. | Section 5. |
| 25 & 26 Vict. c. 53. | The Land Registry Act 1862. | Section 116. |
| 27 & 28 Vict. c. 114. | The Improvement of Land Act 1864. | Section 24. |
| 29 & 30 Vict. c. 122. | The Metropolitan Commons Act 1866. | Section 28. |
| 31 & 32 Vict. c. 109. | The Compulsory Church Rate Abolition Act 1868. | Section 7. |
| 36 & 37 Vict. c. 50. | The Places of Worship Sites Act 1873. | Sections 1 and 3. |
| 40 & 41 Vict. c. 59. | The Colonial Stock Act 1877. | Section 6. |
| 57 & 58 Vict. c. 60. | The Merchant Shipping Act 1894. | In section 55, subsection (1). |

## SCHEDULE 4

Section 148.

### CONSEQUENTIAL AMENDMENTS

1 In the Fines and Recoveries Act 1833—

(a) in section 33 for the words " the Mental Health Act 1959 " and " Part VIII" there shall be substituted respectively the words " the Mental Health Act 1983 " and " Part VII" ;

(b) in sections 48 and 49 for the references to the judge having jurisdiction under Part VIII of the Mental Health Act 1959 there shall be substituted references to the judge having jurisdiction under Part VII of this Act

2 In section 68 of the Improvement of Land Act 1864 for the words " Part VIII of the Mental Health Act 1959 " there shall be substituted the words " Part VII of the Mental Health Act 1983 " .

3 In section 10(3) of the Colonial Prisoners Removal Act 1884 for the words " section seventy-one of the Mental Health Act 1959 ", "section seventy-two" and "section seventy-four" there shall be substituted respectively the words " section 46 of the Mental Health Act 1983 ", " section 47 " and " section 49 ".

4 In the Trustee Act 1925—

(a) in section 36(9) for the words "the Mental Health Act 1959 " and " Part VIII of the Mental Health Act 1959 " there shall be substituted respectively the words " the Mental Health Act 1983 " and " Part VII of the Mental Health Act 1983 ";

(b) in section 41(1) for the words "the Mental Health Act 1959" there shall be substituted the words " the Mental Health Act 1983 " ;

(c) in section 54—

(i) in subsection (1) for the words " Part VIII of the Mental Health Act 1959 " there shall be substituted the words " Part VII of the Mental Health Act 1983 " ; and

(ii) in subsection (3) for the words " section one hundred and one of the Mental Health Act 1959" and " exercisable and have been exercised under section one hundred and four " there shall be substituted respectively the words " section 94 of the Mental Health Act 1983 and " exercisable under section 98 of that Act and have been exercised under that section or section 104 of the Mental Health Act 1959 " ;"

(d) in section 55 except so far as it applies to existing orders made before the commencement of this Act, for the words " Part VIII of the Mental Health Act 1959 " there shall be substituted the words " Part VII of the Mental Health Act 1983 " .

5 In the Law of Property Act 1925—

(a) in section 22(1) for the words " Part VIII of the Mental Health Act 1959 " there shall be substituted the words " Part VII of the Mental Health Act 1983 " ;

(b) in section 205(1)(xiii) for the words "section four of the Mental Health Act 1959 " and " Part VIII" there shall be substituted respectively the words " section 1 of the Mental Health Act 1983 " and " Part VIII of the Mental Health Act 1959 or Part VII of the said Act of 1983 ".

6 In section 111 of the Land Registration Act 1925—

(a) in subsection (5) for the words "the Mental Health Act 1959" and "Part VIII of the Mental Health Act 1959" there shall be substituted respectively the words " the Mental Health Act 1983 " and " Part VII of the Mental Health Act 1983 " ; and

(b) in subsection (6) for the words "Part VIII of the Mental Health Act 1959 " there shall be substituted the words " Part VII of the Mental Health Act 1983 " .

7 In paragraph (ii) of the proviso to section 41(1) of the Administration of Estates Act 1925 for the words "the Mental Health Act 1959" there shall be substituted the words " the Mental Health Act 1983 " .

8 In sections 4(1) and 11(3)(b) of the Polish Resettlement Act 1947 for the words "the Mental Health Act 1959 " there shall be substituted the words " the Mental Health Act 1983 " .

9 In section 1(4) of the U.S.A. Veterans' Pensions (Administration) Act 1949 after the words "curator bonis" there shall be inserted the words " or for whom a receiver has been appointed under section 105 of the Mental Health Act 1959 or section 99 of the Mental Health Act 1983 " .

10 In section 116(7) of the Army Act 1955 for the words "section 71 of the Mental Health Act 1959 " and "within the meaning of the Mental Health Act 1959 " there shall be substituted respectively the words " section 46 of the Mental Health Act 1983 " and " within the meaning of the Mental Health Act 1983 ".

11 In section 116(7) of the Air Force Act 1955 for the words "section 71 of the Mental Health Act 1959" and "within the meaning of the Mental Health Act 1959 " there shall be substituted respectively the words " section 46 of the Mental Health Act Act 1983 " and "within the meaning of the Mental Health Act 1983 ".

12 In section 38(4) of the Sexual Offences Act 1956 for the words " the Mental Health Act 1959 " there shall be substituted the words " the Mental Health Act 1983 " .

13 In section 71(6) of the Naval Discipline Act 1957 for the words " section 71 of the Mental Health Act 1959 " and " within the meaning of the Mental Health Act 1959 " there shall be substituted respectively the words " section 46 of the Mental Health Act 1983 " and " within the meaning of the Mental Health Act 1983 ".

14 In section 1 of the Variation of Trusts Act 1958—

(a) in subsection (3) for the words "Part VIII of the Mental Health Act 1959 " and " the said Part VIII" there shall be substituted respectively the words " Part VII of the Mental Health Act 1983 " and " the said Part VII" ; and

(b) in subsection (6) for the words "Part VIII of the Mental Health Act 1959" there shall be substituted the words " Part VII of the Mental Health Act 1983 " .

15 In section 128(1)(b) of the Mental Health Act 1959 for the words " this Act" in both places where they occur there shall be substituted the words " the Mental Health Act 1983 " .

16 In the Mental Health (Scotland) Act 1960—

(a) in section 10(1)(b) and (c) for the words " the Mental Health Act 1959" there shall be substituted the words " the Mental Health Act 1983 " ;

(b) in section 73(5) for the words " Part IV of the Mental Health Act 1959" there shall be substituted the words " Part II of the Mental Health Act 1983 " ;

(c) in section 75 for the words " Part IV of the Mental Health Act 1959 ", " section forty-nine of the said Act of 1959 ", " Part IV of that Act", " Part TV of the said Act of 1959 ", and " section fifty-two " wherever they occur there shall be substituted respectively the words " Part II of the Mental Health Act 1983 " , " section 26 of the said Act of 1983 ", " Part II of that Act", " Part II of the said Act of 1983 " and " section 29 " ;

(d) in section 76—

(i) in subsection (1) for the words " the Mental Health Act 1959 as amended by this Act" and "Part IV of that Act" there shall be substituted respectively the words " the Mental Health Act 1983 " and " Part II of that Act" ;

(ii) in subsection (2) for the words " sections forty-nine to fifty-one of the said Act of 1959 " and " Part IV of that Act" there shall be substituted respectively the words " sections 26 to 28 of the said Act of 1983 " and " Part II of that Act" ; and

(iii) in subsection (3) after the words " the Mental Health Act 1959 " there shall be inserted the words " or section 29 or 30 of the Mental Health Act 1983 " .

(e) in section 83(3)(a) for the words " mental welfare officer within the meaning of the Mental Health Act 1959 " there shall be substituted the words " approved social worker within the meaning of the Mental Health Act 1983 " ;

(f) in sections 85 and 87 for the words " the Mental Health Act 1959 " there shall be substituted the words " the Mental Health Act 1983 " .

(g) in section 88(2) after " 1959 " there shall be inserted the words " or Part VI of the Mental Health Act 1983 " ;

(h) in section 103(3) and (5) for the words " section ninety-three of the Mental Health Act 1959 " there shall be substituted the words " section 88 of the Mental Health Act 1983 " ;

(i) in section 107(2) for the words " section one hundred and forty-one of the Mental Health Act 1959" there shall be substituted the words " section 139 of the Mental Health Act 1983 " .

17 In section 5 of the Administration of Justice Act 1960—

(a) in subsection (4) for the words " Part V of the Mental Health Health Act 1959 " and the words " the said Part V " there shall be substituted respectively the words " Part III of the Mental Health Act 1983 (other than under section 35, 36 or 38) and " the said Part III " ; and"

(b) in subsection (4A) for the words " section 31 of the Mental Health (Amendment) Act 1982 ", " Part V of the said Act of 1959 " and " the said section 31 " there shall be substituted respectively " section 38 of the Mental Health Act 1983 " , " Part III of the said Act of 1983 " and " the said section 38".

18 In the Criminal Procedure (Insanity) Act 1964—

(a) in section 8(2) for the words " the Mental Health Act 1959 ", " Part V " and " sections 139 to 141 " there shall be substituted respectively the words " the Mental Health Act 1983 " , " Part III" and " sections 137 to 139 " ;

(b) in Schedule 1—

(i) in paragraph 1(3) for the words " sections 60 and 65 of the Mental Health Act 1959" there shall be substituted the words " sections 37 and 41 of the Mental Health Act 1983 " ;

(ii) in paragraph 2(1) for the words " the Mental Health Act 1959 ", " section 60 " and " section 65 " there shall be substituted respectively " the Mental Health Act 1983 " , " section 37 " and " section 41 " ;

(iii) in paragraph 2(2) for the words " section 66 of the said Act of 1959" and "section 65" there shall be substituted respectively the words " section 42 of the said Act of 1983 " and " section 41 " ;

(iv) in paragraph 2(3) for the words " section 63(5) of the Mental Health Act 1959 " and the words from " the proviso " to " the reference " there shall be substituted respectively the words " section 40(5) of the Mental Health Act 1983 " and " the reference in the said section 40(5) " ;

19 In section 18 of the Administration of Justice Act 1965 for the words " Part VIII of the Mental Health Act 1959 " there shall be substituted the words " Part VII of the Mental Health Act 1983 " .

20 In paragraph 1(2)(b) of Schedule 1 to the Compulsory Purchase Act 1965 at the end there shall be inserted the words " or section 98 of the Mental Health Act 1983 " .

21 In the Criminal Justice Act 1967—

(a) in section 72(1)(b) for the words " section 40 or 140 of the Mental Health Act 1959 or section 31(8) of the Mental Health (Amendment) Act 1982 " there shall be substituted the words " section 18, 38(7) or 138 of the Mental Health Act 1983 " ;

(b) in section 72(3) for the words " Section 139 of the Mental Health Act 1959 " and " the said Act of 1959 " there shall be substituted respectively the words " Section 137 of the Mental Health Act 1983 " and " the said Act of 1983 " ;

(c) in section 72(4) for the words " Part V of the Mental Health Act 1959 ", "section 31 of the Mental Health (Amendment) Act 1982 " and " Part V of the said Act of 1959 " there shall be substituted respectively the words " Part III of the Mental Health Act 1983 " , " section 38 of the said Act of 1983 " and " Part III of the said Act of 1983 ".

22 In section 26(2) of the Leasehold Reform Act 1967 for the words " the Mental Health Act 1959 ", " appointed under Part VIII of that Act " and " having jurisdiction under Part VIII of that Act " there shall be substituted respectively the words " Mental Health Act 1983 " , "appointed under Part VII of the said Act of 1983 or Part VIII of the Mental Health Act 1959 " and " having jurisdiction under Part VII of the said Act of 1983 ".

23 In the Criminal Appeal Act 1968—

(a) in section 6(4) for the words " section 72 of the Mental Health Act 1959 " and " subsection (6) " there shall be substituted respectively the words " section 47 of the Mental Health Act 1983 " and " subsection (5) " ;

(b) in section 8(3) after the words " Part V of the Mental Health Act 1959" there shall be inserted the words " or under Part III of the Mental Health Act 1983 (other than under section 35, 36 or 38 of that Act) " ;

(c) in section 8(3A)—

(i) for the words " section 30 of the Mental Health (Amendment) Act 1982" there shall be substituted the words " section 36 of the Mental Health Act 1983 " ;

(ii) for the words " section 31 of that Act" there shall be substituted the words " section 38 of that Act " ; and

(iii) for the words " Part V of the Mental Health Act 1959 " there shall be substituted the words " Part III of that Act " ;

(d) in section 11—

(i) in subsection (5) for the words "the Mental Health (Amendment) Act 1982 " there shall be substituted the words " the Mental Health Act 1983 " ; and

(ii) in subsection (6)(b) for the words " section 31(8) of the said Act of 1982" there shall be substituted the words " section 38(7) of the said Act of 1983 " .

(e) in section 14(5) for the words " section 72 of the Mental Health Act 1959" and "subsection (6)" there shall be substituted respectively the words " section 47 of the Mental Health Act 1983 " and " subsection (5) " ;

(f) in section 16(3) for the words " the Mental Health Act 1959 " and " Part V " there shall be substituted respectively the words " the Mental Health Act 1983 " and " Part III " ;

(g) in section 37(4) for the words " Part V of the Mental Health Act 1959 " and " the Mental Health Act 1959 " there shall be substituted respectively the words " Part III of the Mental Health Act 1983 (otherwise than under section 35, 36 or 38 of that Act) " and "the Mental Health Act 1983 " ;

(h) in section 37(4A) for the words " section 30 of the Mental Health (Amendment) Act 1982 ", " section 31 " and " Part V of the said Act of 1959 " wherever they occur there shall be substituted respectively the words " section 36 of the Mental Health Act 1983 " , " section 38 " and " Part III of the said Act of 1983 " ;

(i) in section 50(1), for the words from "Part V" to " 1982" there shall be substituted the words " Part III of the Mental Health Act 1983, with or without a restriction order, and an interim hospital order under that Part " ;

(j) in section 51(2) for the words " section 147(1) of the Mental Health Act 1959 " there shall be substituted the words " section 145(1) of the Mental Health Act 1983 " ;

(k) in paragraph 1(3) of Schedule 1 for the words " the Mental Health Act 1959 " there shall be substituted the words " the Mental Health Act 1983 " ;

(l) in paragraph 2 of Schedule 1 for the words " the Mental Health Act 1959 ", " section 60 " and " section 65 " there shall be substituted respectively the words " the Mental Health Act 1983 " , " section 37 " and " section 41 " ;

(m) in paragraph 3 of Schedule 1 for the words " Part IV of the Mental Health Act 1959 " and " the said Part IV" there shall be substituted respectively the words " Part II of the Mental Health Act 1983 " and " the said Part II " ;

(n) in Schedule 3—

(i) in the heading to the Schedule for the words " PART V OF MENTAL HEALTH ACT 1959 " there shall be substituted the words " PART II OF MENTAL HEALTH ACT 1983 " ; and

(ii) for paragraph 2 there shall be substituted—

*"Order for continued detention under Act of 1983*

2 Where an order is made by the Court of Appeal under section 16(3) of this Act for a person's continued detention under the Mental Health Act 1983, Part III of that Act (patients concerned in criminal proceedings or under sentence) shall apply to him as if he had been ordered under the said section 16(3) to be kept in custody pending trial and were detained in pursuance of a transfer direction together with a restriction direction.".

24 In the Courts-Martial (Appeals) Act 1968—

(a) in sections 20(4) and 43(4) for the words " Part V of the Mental Health Act 1959" there shall be substituted the words " Part III of the Mental Health Act 1983 " ;

(b) in section 23, in subsection (1) for the words " section 71 of the Mental Health Act 1959 " there shall be substituted the words " section 46 of the Mental Health Act 1983 " and in subsection (2) for the words " the Mental Health Act 1959 " there shall be substituted the words " the Mental Health Act 1983 " ;

(c) in section 25(4) for the words " the Mental Health Act 1959 " there shall be substituted the words " the Mental Health Act 1983 " .

25 In section 21(4) of the Family Law Reform Act 1969 for the words " the Mental Health Act 1959 " there shall be substituted the words " the Mental Health Act 1983 " .

26 In the Children and Young Persons Act 1969—

(a) in section 1(3) for the words " Part V of the Mental Health Act 1959" there shall be substituted the words " Part III of the Mental Health Act 1983 " ;

(b) in section 1(5) for the words " section 60 of the said Act of 1959 " there shall be substituted the words " section 37 of the said Act of 1983 " ;

(c) in section 2(10) for the words " section 31 of the Mental Health (Amendment) Act 1982" and "the said section 31 " there shall be substituted respectively the words " section 38 of the Mental Health Act 1983 " and " the said section 38".

(d) in section 12(4) for the words " section 28 of the Mental Health Act 1959 ", " Part V " and " the said Act of 1959 " there shall be substituted respectively the words " section 12 of the Mental Health Act 1983 " , " Part III" and " the said Act of 1983 " ;

(e) in paragraph 7(7) of Schedule 4 for the words from the beginning to " 1959 " there shall be substituted the words " A restriction direction which was given under section 49 of the Mental Health Act 1983 " .

27 In Schedule 1 to the Local Authorities Social Services Act 1970—

(a) in the entry relating to the Mental Health Act 1959, in the first column for the words " Parts II to VI and IX " there shall be substituted the words " sections 8 and 9 " and for the entry in the second column there shall be substituted the words " Welfare and accommodation of mentally disordered persons. " ;

(b) there shall be inserted at the end—

| "Mental Health Act 1983 (c. 20) | |
|---|---|
| Parts II, III and VI | Welfare of the mentally disordered; guardianship of persons suffering from mental disorder including such persons removed to England and Wales from Scotland or Northern Ireland; exercise of functions of nearest relative of person so suffering. |
| Sections 66, 67, 69(1) | Exercise of functions of nearest relative in relation to applications and references to Mental Health Review Tribunals. |
| Section 114 | Appointment of approved social workers. |
| Section 115 | Entry and inspection. |
| Section 116 | Welfare of certain hospital patients. |
| Section 117 | After-care of detained patients. |
| Section 130 | Prosecutions.". |

(c) the entry relating to the Mental Health (Amendment) Act 1982 shall cease to have effect.

28 In section 57(1) of the Courts Act 1971 for the words " Part V of the Mental Health Act 1959" there shall be substituted the words " Part III of the Mental Health Act 1983 " .

29 In Schedule 1 to the Tribunals and Inquiries Act 1971, in the second column of the entry relating to the Mental Health Review Tribunals for the words following " Tribunals " there shall be substituted the words " constituted or having effect as if constituted under section 65 of the Mental Health Act 1983 (c. 20) " .

30 In section 30(2) of the Immigration Act 1971 for the words from the beginning to " I960)" there shall be substituted the words " Under section 82 of the Mental Health (Scotland) Act 1960 " and the words from " and accordingly " onwards shall be omitted.

31 In section 20(2) of the Parliamentary and other Pensions Act 1972 for the words "Section 138 of the Mental Health Act 1959" there shall be substituted the words " Section 142 of the Mental Health Act 1983 " .

32 In section 118 of the Local Government Act 1972—

(a) in subsection (1) for the words "the Mental Health Act 1959 " there shall be substituted the words " the Mental Health Act 1983 " ; and

(b) in subsection (4) for the words " Part VIII of the said Act of 1959 " there shall be substituted the words " Part VII of the said Act of 1983 " .

33 In the Costs in Criminal Cases Act 1973—

(a) in section 3(7) for the words from "under Part V" to " 1982" there shall be substituted the words " and an interim hospital order under Part III of the Mental Health Act 1983 " ; and

(b) in section 18(1)(c) for the words "Part V of the Mental Health Act 1959" there shall be substituted the words " Part III of the Mental Health Act 1983 " .

34 In section 12(d) of the Matrimonial Causes Act 1973 for the words "the Mental Health Act 1959" there shall be substituted the words " the Mental Health Act 1983 " .

35 In section 1 of the Guardianship Act 1973—

(a) in subsection (8), the words from " and" to the end of the subsection shall be omitted; and

(b) after subsection (8) there shall be inserted—

> "(9) Nothing in this section shall be taken to affect the provisions of the Mental Health Act 1983 as to the person who is ' the nearest relative' for the purposes of that Act.".

36 In section 3 of the Powers of Criminal Courts Act 1973—

(a) in subsection (1) for the words " section 28 of the Mental Health Act 1959 " and " Part V of that Act" there shall be substituted respectively the words " section 12 of the Mental Health Act 1983 " and " Part III of that Act " ;

(b) in subsection (2) for the words " hospital or mental nursing home within the meaning of the Mental Health Act 1959 " and " that Act" there shall be substituted respectively the words " hospital within the meaning of the Mental Health Act 1983 or mental nursing home within the meaning of the Nursing Homes Act 1975 " and " the National Health Service Act 1977 " ; and

(c) in subsection (7) for the words "Subsections (2) and (3) of section 62 of the Mental Health Act 1959 " and " section 60(1)(a)" there shall be substituted respectively the words " Subsections (2) and (3) of section 54 of the Mental Health Act 1983 " and " section 37(2)(a) ".

37 In Group D in Schedule 1 to the Juries Act 1974 for the words " section 33 of the Mental Health Act 1959 ", " Part VIII of that Act" and " the said Act of 1959 " there shall be substituted respectively the words " section 7 of the Mental Health Act 1983 " , " Part VII of that Act " and " the said Act of 1983 ".

38 In the Solicitors Act 1974—

(a) in section 12(1)(j) for the words " section 101 of the Mental Health Act 1959 " and " section 104 of that Act" there shall be substituted respectively the words " section 94 of the Mental Health Act 1983 " and " section 104 of the Mental Health Act 1959 or section 98 of the said Act of 1983 " ;

(b) in section 62(4)(c) for the words " under Part VIII of the Mental Health Act 1959" there shall be substituted the words " appointed under Part VII of the Mental Health Act 1983 " ;

(c) in paragraph 1(1)(f) of Schedule 1 for the words "section 104 (emergency powers) or 105 (appointment of receiver) of the Mental Health Act 1959 " there shall be substituted the words " section 104 of the Mental Health Act 1959 or section 98 of the Mental Health Act 1983 (emergency powers) or section 105 of the said Act of 1959 or section 99 of the said Act of 1983 (appointment of receiver) " .

39 In section 5(7) of the Rehabilitation of Offenders Act 1974 for the words " Part V of the Mental Health Act 1959 " there shall be substituted the words " Part III of the Mental Health Act 1983 " .

40 In paragraph 19(4) of Schedule 5 to the Finance Act 1975 for the words " the Mental Health Act 1959 " there shall be substituted the words " the Mental Health Act 1983 " .

41 In the Criminal Procedure (Scotland) Act 1975—

(a) in sections 13(1)(b) and 322(1)(b) for the words " section 40 or 140 of the Mental Health Act 1959, section 31(8) of the Mental Health (Amendment) Act 1982 " there shall be substituted the words " section 18, 38(7) or 138 of the Mental Health Act 1983 " ;

(b) in sections 13(3) and 322(3) for the words "Section 139 of the Mental Health Act 1959 " and " the said Act of 1959 " there shall be substituted respectively " Section 137 of the Mental Health Act 1983 " and " the said Act of 1983 " ;

(c) in sections 13(4) and 322(4) for the words "Part V of the Mental Health Act 1959 "," section 31 of the Mental Health (Amendment) Act 1982 " and " Part V of the said Act of 1959" there shall be substituted respectively the words " Part III of the Mental Health Act 1983 " , " section 38 of the said Act of 1983 " and " Part III of the said Act of 1983 ".

42 In Part II of Schedule 1 to the House of Commons Disqualification Act 1975 in the entry relating to Mental Health Review Tribunals for the words "constituted under the Mental Health Act 1959" there shall be substituted the words " constituted or having effect as if constituted under the Mental Health Act 1983 " .

43 In the Nursing Homes Act 1975—

(a) in sections 3(2)(c) and 10(2) for the words "the Mental Health Act 1959 or the Mental Health (Amendment) Act 1982" there shall be substituted the words " the Mental Health Act 1983 " ;

(b) in section 20(1) for the words " section 4 of the Mental Health Act 1959" there shall be substituted the words " section 1 of the Mental Health Act 1983 " ;

(c) in section 21 for the words " those sections" there shall be substituted the words " the sections of the Mental Health Act 1983 corresponding to those sections, namely sections 126, 139 and 125 respectively " .

44 In section 98(4) of the Children Act 1975 for the words " or residential home within the meaning of Part III of the Mental Health Act 1959 " there shall be substituted the words " residential home for mentally disordered persons within the meaning of the Nursing Homes Act 1975 or the Residential Homes Act 1980 " .

45 In section 32(6)(c) of the Adoption Act 1976 for the words " the Mental Health Act 1959 or the Mental Health (Amendment) Act 1982 " there shall be substituted the words " the Mental Health Act 1983 " .

46 In section 3(6B) of the Bail Act 1976 for the words " section 28 of the Mental Health Act 1959 " there shall be substituted the words " section 12 of the Mental Health Act 1983 " .

47 In the National Health Service Act 1977—

(a) in section 4 for the words " the Mental Health Act 1959 or the Mental Health (Amendment) Act 1982 " there shall be substituted the words " the Mental Health Act 1983 " ;

(b) in section 105(1) for the words " Part IV of the Mental Health Act 1959" there shall be substituted the words " Part II of the Mental Health Act 1983 " ;

(c) in section 105(3) the words " or the Mental Health Act 1959 " shall be omitted ;

(d) in section 128(1), in the definition of " illness ", for the words " the Mental Health Act 1959 " there shall be substituted the words " the Mental Health Act 1983 " ;

(e) in paragraph 2 of Schedule 8—

(i) for sub-paragraph (1)(d) there shall be substituted—

"(d) for the exercise of the functions of the authority in respect of persons suffering from mental disorder who are received into guardianship under Part II or III of the Mental Health Act 1983 (whether the guardianship of the local social services authority or of other persons).";

(ii) in sub-paragraph (2)(b)(i) for the words " the Mental Health Act 1959 " there shall be substituted the words " the Mental Health Act 1983 " ; and

(iii) in sub-paragraph (3) for the words " that Act of 1959 " there shall be substituted the words " that Act of 1983 " ;

(f) in paragraph 13(1)(b) of Schedule 14 for the words " 80 to 83, 86 to 91, 93 and 96 " there shall be substituted " 80 to 82, 96 " .

48 In section 16A(1)(b)(ii) of the National Health Service (Scotland) Act 1978 for the words " section 10 of the Mental Health Act 1959 " there shall be substituted the words " section 116 of the Mental Health Act 1983 " .

49 In paragraph 5(2) of Schedule 1 to the Capital Gains Tax Act 1979 for the words " the Mental Health Act 1959 " there shall be substituted the words " the Mental Health Act 1983 " .

50 In the Child Care Act 1980—

(a) in section 3(1)(b)(iii) for the words " the Mental Health Act 1959" there shall be substituted the words " the Mental Health Act 1983 " ; and

(b) in section 79(5)(c) for the words " section 10 of that Act" and " subsection (1)(a)" there shall be substituted respectively the words " section 116 of the Mental Health Act 1983 " and " subsection (2)(a) ".

51 In section 2(5) of the Foster Children Act 1980 for the words " the Mental Health Act 1959 or the Mental Health (Amendment) Act 1982 " there shall be substituted the words " the Mental Health Act 1983 " .

52 In the Residential Homes Act 1980—

(a) in section 1(3)(a) for the words " section 147(1) of the Mental Health Act 1959 " there shall be substituted the words " section 145(1) of the Mental Health Act 1983 " ; and

(b) in section 10(1) for the words " the Mental Health Act 1959 " there shall be substituted the words " the Mental Health Act 1983 " .

53 In paragraph 2(a) of Schedule 2 to the Reserve Forces Act 1980 for the words "the Mental Health Act 1959" there shall be substituted the words " the Mental Health Act 1983 " .

54 In section 31(2)(c) of the Transport Act 1980 for the words " Part VIII of the Mental Health Act 1959 " there shall be substituted the words " Part VII of the Mental Health Act 1983 " .

55 In section 38 of the Limitation Act 1980—

(a) in subsection (3) for the words " Mental Health Act 1959 " there shall be substituted the words " Mental Health Act 1983 " ; and

(b) in subsection (4)—

(i) in paragraph (a), for the words " the Mental Health Act 1959 or section 30 or 31 of the Mental Health (Amendment) Act 1982 " there shall be substituted the words " the Mental Health Act 1983 (otherwise than by virtue of section 35 or 89) " ; and

(ii) for paragraph (b) there shall be substituted—

"(b) while he is receiving treatment as an in-patient in any hospital within the meaning of the Mental Health Act 1983 or mental nursing home within the meaning of the Nursing Homes Act 1975 without being liable to be detained under the said Act of 1983 (otherwise than by virtue of section 35 or 89), being treatment which follows without any interval a period during which he was liable to be detained or subject to guardianship under the Mental Health Act 1959, or the said Act of 1983 (otherwise than by virtue of section 35 or 89) or by virtue of any enactment repealed or excluded by the Mental Health Act 1959".

56 In section 57(2)(c) of the Public Passenger Vehicles Act 1981 for the words " Part VIII of the Mental Health Act 1959 " there shall be substituted the words " Part VII of the Mental Health Act 1983 " .

57 In the Contempt of Court Act 1981—

(a) in section 14(4) for the words " section 60 of the Mental Health Act 1959" and "section 31 of the Mental Health (Amendment) Act 1982" there shall be substituted respectively the words " section 37 of the Mental Health Act 1983 " and " section 38 of that Act " ; and

(b) in section 14(4A) for the words " section 29 of the said Act of 1982 " there shall be substituted the words " section 35 of the said Act of 1983 " .

(c) in paragraph 10(b) of Schedule 1 for the words " paragraph (b) of subsection (2) of section 76 of the Mental Health Act 1959" there shall be substituted the words " section 51(5) of the Mental Health Act 1983 " .

58 In the Supreme Court Act 1981—

(a) in section 48(6)(a) for the words "Part V of the Mental Health Act 1959 " and " the Mental Health (Amendment) Act 1982 " there shall be substituted respectively the words " Part III of the Mental Health Act 1983 " and " that Act" ;

(b) in section 48(7) for the words " the said Act of 1982 " there shall be substituted the words " the said Act of 1983 " ; and

(c) in section 48(8)(b) for the words " section 31(8) of the said Act of 1982 " there shall be substituted the words " section 38(7) of the said Act of 1983 " .

59 In section 13(9) of the Armed Forces Act 1981 or the words " the Mental Health Act 1959 " there shall be substituted the words " the Mental Health Act 1983 " .

60 In paragraph 9 of Schedule 1 to the British Nationality Act 1981.—

(a) in sub-paragraph (1)(b) for the words " Part V of the Mental Health Act 1959 " there shall be substituted the words " Part 111 of the Mental Health Act 1983 " ; and

(b) in sub-paragraph (2)(b) for the words " Part V of the Mental Health Act 1959" there shall be substituted the words " Part III of the Mental Health Act 1983 " .

61 In the Mental Health (Amendment) Act 1982—

(a) in section 70(2)—

(i) for the words " Sections 62 and 64(2)" there shall be substituted the words " Section 62 " , and

(ii) the words " sections 35(1) and (2) and 64(6) above extend to Northern Ireland " shall be omitted ;

(b) in section 70(3) for the words " Section 154(2) of the principal Act" there shall be substituted the words " Section 149(4) of the Mental Health Act 1983 " .

## SCHEDULE 5

Section 148.

### Transitional and Saving Provisions

1 Where any period of time specified in an enactment repealed by this Act is current at the commencement of this Act, this Act shall have effect as if the corresponding provision of this Act had been in force when that period began to run.

2 Nothing in this Act shall affect the interpretation of any provision of the Mental Health Act 1959 which is not repealed by this Act and accordingly sections 1 and 145(1) of this Act shall apply to any such provision as if it were contained in this Act.

3 Where, apart from this paragraph, anything done under or for the purposes of any enactment which is repealed by this Act would cease to have effect by virtue of that repeal it shall have effect as if it had been done under or for the purposes of the corresponding provision of this Act.

4 (1) Until the expiration of the period of two years beginning with the day on which the Mental Health (Amendment) Act 1982 was passed this Act shall have effect as if—

(a) section 114 were omitted ;

(b) in section 145(1) the definition of an approved social worker were omitted and there were inserted in the appropriate place the following definition:—

"' mental welfare officer' means an officer of a local social services authority appointed to act as mental welfare officer for the purposes of the Mental Health Act 1959 or this Act";

(c) for paragraph 16(e) of Schedule 4 there were substituted—

"(e) in section 83(3)(a) for the words ' the Mental Health Act 1959' there were substituted the words ' the Mental Health Act 1983 '";

(d) for paragraph 47(e)(i) of Schedule 4 there were substituted—

"(i) in sub-paragraph (1)(d) for the words ' the Mental Health Act 1959' and ' Part IV or Part V' there were substituted respectively the words ' the Mental Health Act 1983 ' and ' Part II or III ';"and

(e) for any reference to an approved social worker there were substituted a reference to a mental welfare officer.

(2) Any appointment of a person as a mental welfare officer for the purposes of the Mental Health Act 1959 or this Act shall terminate at the expiration of the period mentioned in sub-paragraph (1) above but without prejudice to anything previously done by that person or to the continuation by an approved social worker of anything which is then in process of being done by that person.

5 If no order has been made under section 11 of the National Health Service Act 1977 before 30th September 1983 establishing the Mental Health Act Commission the following shall be substituted for subsection (1) of section 121 of this Act—

"(1) The Secretary of State shall under section 11 of the National Health Service Act 1977 establish a special health authority to be known as the Mental Health Act Commission.".

6 This Act shall apply in relation to any authority for the detention or guardianship of a person who was liable to be detained or subject to guardianship under the Mental Health Act 1959 immediately before 30th September 1983 as if the provisions of this Act which derive from provisions amended by section 1 or 2 of the Mental Health (Amendment) Act 1982 and the amendments in Schedule 3 to that Act which are consequential on those sections were included in this Act in the form the provisions from which they derive would take if those amendments were disregarded but this provision shall not apply to any renewal of that authority on or after that date.

7 This Act shall apply to any application made before 30th September 1983 as if the provisions of this Act which derive from provisions amended by sections 3 to 5 of the Mental Health (Amendment) Act 1982 and the amendments in Schedule 3 to that Act which are consequential on those sections were included in this Act in the form the provisions from which they derive would take if those amendments were disregarded.

8 (1) Where on 30th September 1983 a person who has not attained the age of sixteen years is subject to guardianship by virtue of a guardianship application the authority for his guardianship shall terminate on that day.

(2) Section 8(1) of this Act has effect (instead of section 34(1) of the Mental Health Act 1959) in relation to a guardianship application made before the coming into force of this Act as well as in relation to one made later.

9 (1) Section 20(1) of this Act shall have effect in relation to any application for admission for treatment and to any guardianship application made before 1st October 1983 with the substitution for the words " six months" of the words "one year".

(2) Section 20(2) of this Act shall have effect in relation to any authority renewed before 1st October 1983 with the substitution for the words " six months " of the words " one year " and for the words "one year" in both places they occur of the words "two years ".

(3) Where an authority has been renewed on or before 30th September 1983 for a period of two years of which less than 16 months has expired on that date that period shall expire at the end of 18 months from the date on which it began,

10 Section 23(2)(a) of this Act shall have effect in relation to a patient liable to be detained in pursuance of an application under section 25 of the Mental Health Act 1959 made before 30th September 1983 as if the reference to the nearest relative of the patient were omitted.

11 Where at any time before 30th September 1983 an application to a Mental Health Review Tribunal has been made by a person who at that time was the patient's nearest relative and the application has not then been determined and by reason of the coming into force of section 26 of this Act that person ceased to be the patient's nearest relative on that date, that person shall nevertheless be treated for the purposes of the application as continuing to be his nearest relative.

12 A person—

(a) who was admitted to hospital in pursuance of an application for admission for treatment; or

(b) in respect of whom a guardianship application was accepted ; or

(c) in respect of whom a hospital order was made,

before 30th September 1983 may make an application to a tribunal under section 66 of this Act in the cases mentioned in subsection (1)(b) and (c) of that section and under section 69(1)(b) of this Act within the period of six months beginning with the day on which he attains the age of 16 years if that period is later than that which would otherwise apply to an application in his case.

13 Subsection (1) of section 68 of this Act does not apply to any patient admitted or transferred to hospital more than six months before 30th September 1983 ; and subsection (2) of that section applies only in relation to a renewal of authority for detention after that date.

14 Section 69(1)(b) of this Act shall have effect in relation Ito patients liable to be detained immediately before 30th September 1983 as if after the words " in respect of a patient" there were inserted the words " admitted to a hospital in pursuance of a hospital order or " .

15 The provisions of this Act which derive from sections 24 to 27 of the Mental Health (Amendment) Act 1982 shall have effect in relation to a transfer direction given before 30th September 1983 as well as in relation to one given later, but where, apart from this paragraph, a transfer direction given before 30th September 1983 would by virtue of the words in section 50(3) of this Act which are derived from section 24(3) of the Mental Health (Amendment) Act 1982 have ceased to have effect before that date it shall cease to have effect on that date.

16 The words in section 42(1) of this Act which derive from the amendment of section 66(1) of the Mental Health Act 1959 by section 28(1) of the Mental Health (Amendment) Act 1982 and the provisions of this Act which derive from section 28(3) of and Schedule 1 to that Act have effect in relation to a restriction order or, as the case may be, a restriction direction made or given before 30th September 1983 as well as in relation to one made or given later, but—

(a) any reference to a tribunal under section 66(6) of the said Act of 1959 in respect of a patient shall be treated for the purposes of subsections (1) and (2) of section 77 of this Act in their application to sections 70 and 75(2) of this Act as an application made by him ; and

(b) sections 71(5) and 75(1)(a) of this Act do not apply where the period in question has expired before 30th September 1983.

17 Section 91(2) of this Act shall not apply in relation to a patient removed from England and Wales before 30th September 1983.

18 (1) Subsection (3) of section 58 of this Act shall not apply to any treatment given to a patient in the period of six months beginning with 30th September 1983 if—

(a) the detention of the patient began before the beginning of that period; and

(b) that subsection has not been complied with in respect of any treatment previously given to him in that period.

(2) The Secretary of State may by order reduce the length of the period mentioned in sub-paragraph (1) above.

19 In the case of a patient who is detained at the time when section 132 of this Act comes into force, the steps required by that section shall be taken as soon as practicable after that time.

20 The repeal by the Mental Health (Amendment) Act 1982 of section 77 of the Mental Health Act 1959 does not affect subsection (4) of that section in its application to a transfer direction given before 30th September 1983, but after the coming into force of this Act that subsection shall have effect for that purpose as if for the references to subsection (6) of section 60, Part IV of that Act and the provisions of that Act there were substituted respectively references to section 37(8), Part II and the provisions of this Act.

21 Section 46(3) of this Act shall apply to any direction to which section 71(4) of the Mental Health Act 1959 applied immediately before the commencement of this Act.

22 Notwithstanding the repeal by this Act of section 53(5) of the Mental Health Act 1959, the discharge or variation under that section of an order made under section 52 of that Act shall not affect the validity of anything previously done in pursuance of the order.

23 For any reference in any enactment, instrument, deed or other document to a receiver under Part VIII of the Mental Health Act 1959 there shall be substituted a reference to a receiver under Part VII of this Act.

24 Nothing in this Act shall affect the operation of the proviso to section 107(5) of the Mental Health Act 1959 in relation to a charge created before the commencement of this Act under that section.

25 Nothing in this Act shall affect the operation of subsection (6) of section 112 of the Mental Health Act 1959 in relation to a charge created before the commencement of this Act by virtue of subsection (5) of that section.

26 If the person who is the Master of the Court of Protection at the commencement of this Act has before that time duly taken the oaths required by section 115(1) of the Mental Health Act 1959 he shall not be obliged to take those oaths again by virtue of section 93(3) of this Act.

27 Nothing in this Act shall affect the operation of section 116 of the Mental Health Act 1959 in relation to orders made, directions or authorities given or other instruments issued before the commencement of this Act.

28 References to applications, recommendations, reports and other documents in section 126 of this Act shall include those to which section 125 of the Mental Health Act 1959 applied immediately before the commencement of this Act and references

in section 139 of this Act to the acts to which that section applies shall include those to which section 141 of the said Act of 1959 applied at that time.

29 The repeal by the Mental Health Act 1959 of the Mental Treatment Act 1930 shall not affect any amendment effected by section 20 of that Act in any enactment not repealed by the said Act of 1959.

30 The repeal by the Mental Health Act 1959 of the provisions of the Lunacy Act 1890 and of the Mental Deficiency Act 1913 relating to the superannuation of officers or employees shall not affect any arrangements for the payment of allowances or other benefits made in accordance with those provisions and in force on 1st November 1960.

31 (1) Any patient who immediately before the commencement of this Act was liable to be detained in a hospital or subject to guardianship by virtue of paragraph 9 of Schedule 6 to the Mental Health Act 1959 shall unless previously discharged continue to be so liable for the remainder of the period of his treatment current on 1st November 1960.

(2) The patient may before the expiration of the period of treatment referred to in sub-paragraph (1) above apply to a Mental Health Review Tribunal.

32 Any patient who immediately before the commencement of this Act was liable to be detained or subject to guardianship by virtue of an authority which had been renewed under paragraph 11 of Schedule 6 to the Mental Health Act 1959 shall unless previously discharged continue to be so liable during the period for which that authority was so renewed.

33 (1) This paragraph applies to patients who at the commencement of this Act are liable to be detained or subject to guardianship by virtue of paragraph 31 or 32 above.

(2) Authority for the detention or guardianship of the patient may on the expiration of the relevant period, unless the patient has previously been discharged, be renewed for a further period of two years.

(3) Sections 20(3) to (10) and 66(1)(f) of this Act shall apply in relation to the renewal of authority for the detention or guardianship of a patient under this paragraph as they apply in relation to the renewal of authority for the detention or guardianship of the patient under section 20(2).

(4) In this paragraph " the relevant period " means—

(a) in relation to a patient liable to be detained or subject to guardianship by virtue of the said paragraph 31, the period of his treatment referred to in that paragraph ;

(b) in relation to a patient detained by virtue of the said paragraph 32, the period for which authority for the detention or guardianship of the patient has been renewed under paragraph 11 of Schedule 6 to the 1959 Act;

(c) in relation to a patient the authority for whose detention or guardianship has previously been renewed under this paragraph, the latest period for which it has been so renewed.

34 (1) Any patient who is liable to be detained in a hospital or subject to guardianship by virtue of paragraph 31 above shall (subject to the exceptions and modifications specified in the following provisions of this paragraph) be treated as if he had been admitted to the hospital in pursuance of an application for admission for treatment under Part II of this Act or had been received into guardianship in pursuance of a guardianship application under the said Part II and had been so admitted or received

as a patient suffering from the form or forms of mental disorder recorded under paragraph 7 of Schedule 6 to the Mental Health Act 1959 or, if a different form or forms have been specified in a report under section 38 of that Act as applied by that paragraph, the form or forms so specified.

(2) Section 20 of this Act shall not apply in relation to the patient, but the provisions of paragraph 33 above shall apply instead.

(3) Any patient to whom paragraph 9(3) of Schedule 6 to the Mental Health Act 1959 applied at the commencement of this Act who fell within paragraph (b) of that paragraph shall cease to be liable to be detained on attaining the age of 25 years unless, during the period of two months ending on the date when he attains that age, the responsible medical officer records his opinion under the following provisions of this Schedule that the patient is unfit for discharge.

(4) If the patient was immediately before 1st November 1960 liable to be detained by virtue of section 6, 8(1) or 9 of the Mental Deficiency Act 1913, the power of discharging him under section 23 of this Act shall not be exercisable by his nearest relative, but his nearest relative may make one application in respect of him to a Mental Health Review Tribunal in any period of 12 months.

35 (1) The responsible medical officer may record for the purposes of paragraph 34(3) above his opinion that a patient detained in a hospital is unfit for discharge if it appears to the responsible medical officer—

(a) that if that patient were released from the hospital he would be likely to act in a manner dangerous to other persons or to himself, or would be likely to resort to criminal activities ; or

(b) that that patient is incapable of caring for himself and that there is no suitable hospital or other establishment into which he can be admitted and where he would be likely to remain voluntarily;

and where the responsible medical officer records his opinion as aforesaid he shall also record the grounds for his opinion.

(2) Where the responsible medical officer records his opinion under this paragraph in respect of a patient, the managers of the hospital or other persons in charge of the establishment where he is for the time being detained or liable to be detained shall cause the patient to be informed, and the patient may, at any time before the expiration of the period of 28 days beginning with the date on which he is so informed, apply to a Mental Health Review Tribunal.

(3) On any application under sub-paragraph (2) above the tribunal shall, if satisfied that none of the conditions set out in paragraphs (a) and (b) of sub-paragraph (1) above are fulfilled, direct that the patient be discharged, and subsection (1) of section 72 of this Act shall have effect in relation to the application as if paragraph (b) of that subsection were omitted.

36 Any person who immediately before the commencement of this Act was deemed to have been named as the guardian of any patient under paragraph 14 of Schedule 6 to the Mental Health Act 1959 shall be deemed for the purposes of this Act to have been named as the guardian of the patient in an application for his reception into guardianship under Part II of this Act accepted on that person's behalf by the relevant local authority.

37 (1) This paragraph applies to patients who immediately before the commencement of this Act were transferred patients within the meaning of paragraph 15 of Schedule 6 to the Mental Health Act 1959.

(2) A transferred patient who immediately before the commencement of this Act was by virtue of sub-paragraph (2) of that paragraph treated for the purposes of that Act as if he were liable to be detained in a hospital in pursuance of a direction under section 71 of that Act shall be treated as if he were so liable in pursuance of a direction under section 46 of this Act.

(3) A transferred patient who immediately before the commencement of this Act was by virtue of sub-paragraph (3) of that paragraph treated for the purposes of that Act as if he were liable to be detained in a hospital by virtue of a transfer direction under section 72 of that Act and as if a direction restricting his discharge had been given under section 74 of that Act shall be treated as if he were so liable by virtue of a transfer direction under section 47 of this Act and as if a restriction direction had been given under section 49 of this Act.

(4) Section 84 of this Act shall apply to a transferred patient who was treated by virtue of sub-paragraph (5) of that paragraph immediately before the commencement of this Act as if he had been removed to a hospital under section 89 of that Act as if he had been so removed under the said section 84.

(5) Any person to whom sub-paragraph (6) of that paragraph applied immediately before the commencement of this Act shall be treated for the purposes of this Act as if he were liable to be detained in a hospital in pursuance of a transfer direction given under section 48 of this Act and as if a restriction direction had been given under section 49 of this Act, and he shall be so treated notwithstanding that he is not suffering from a form of mental disorder mentioned in the said section 48.

38 Any patient who immediately before the commencement of this Act was treated by virtue of sub-paragraph (1) of paragraph 16 of Schedule 6 to the Mental Health Act 1959 as if he had been conditionally discharged under section 66 of that Act shall be treated as if he had been conditionally discharged under section 42 of this Act and any such direction as is mentioned in paragraph (b) of that sub-paragraph shall be treated as if it had been given under the said section 42.

39 Upon a restriction direction in respect of a patient who immediately before the commencement of this Act was a transferred patient within the meaning of paragraph 15 of Schedule 6 to the Mental Health Act 1959 ceasing to have effect, the responsible medical officer shall record his opinion whether the patient is suffering from mental illness, severe mental impairment, psychopathic disorder or mental impairment, and references in this Act to the form or forms of mental disorder specified in the relevant application, order or direction shall be construed as including references to the form or forms of mental disorder recorded under this paragraph or under paragraph 17 of the said Schedule 6.

40 A person who immediately before the commencement of this Act was detained by virtue of paragraph 19 of Schedule 6 to the Mental Health Act 1959 may continue to be detained until the expiration of the period of his treatment current on 1st November 1960 or until he becomes liable to be detained or subject to guardianship under this Act, whichever occurs first, and may be so detained in any place in which he might have been detained under that paragraph.

41 Any opinion recorded by the responsible medical officer under the foregoing provisions of this Schedule shall be recorded in such form as may be prescribed by regulations made by the Secretary of State.

42 (1) In the foregoing provisions of this Schedule—

(a) references to the period of treatment of a patient that was current on 1st November 1960 are to the period for which he would have been liable to be detained or subject to guardianship by virtue of any enactment repealed or excluded by the Mental Health Act 1959, or any enactment repealed or replaced by any such enactment as aforesaid, being a period which began but did not expire before that date ; and

(b) " the responsible medical officer " means—

(i) in relation to a patient subject to guardianship, the medical officer authorised by the local social services authority to act (either generally or in any particular case or for any particular purpose) as the responsible medical officer;

(ii) in relation to any other class of patient, the registered medical practitioner in charge of the treatment of the patient.

(2) Subsection (2) of section 34 of this Act shall apply for the purposes of the foregoing provisions of this Schedule as it applies for the purposes of Part II of this Act.

(3) The sentence or other period of detention of a person who was liable to be detained or subject to guardianship immediately before 1st November 1960 by virtue of an order under section 9 of the Mental Deficiency Act 1913 shall be treated for the purposes of the foregoing provisions of this Schedule as expiring at the end of the period for which that person would have been liable to be detained in a prison or other institution if the order had not been made.

(4) For the purposes of the foregoing provisions of this Schedule, an order sending a person to an institution or placing a person under guardianship made before 9th March 1956 on a petition presented under the Mental Deficiency Act 1913 shall be deemed to be valid if it was so deemed immediately before the commencement of this Act by virtue of section 148(2) of the Mental Health Act 1959.

43 (1) Any order or appointment made, direction or authority given, or thing done which by virtue of paragraph 25 of Schedule 6 to the Mental Health Act 1959 had effect immediately before the commencement of this Act as if made, given or done under any provision of Part VIII of that Act shall have effect as if made, given or done under Part VII of this Act.

(2) Where at the commencement of this Act Part VIII of the Mental Health Act 1959 applied in any person's case by virtue of paragraph 25 of Schedule 6 to that Act as if immediately after the commencement of that Act it had been determined that he was a patient within the meaning of the said Part VIII, Part VII of this Act shall apply in his case as if immediately after the commencement of this Act it had been determined that he was a patient within the meaning of the said Part VII.

44 Where a person who immediately before 1st November 1960 was the committee of the estate of a person of unsound mind so found by inquisition was immediately before the commencement of this Act deemed by virtue of paragraph 26 of Schedule 6 to the Mental Health Act 1959 to be a receiver appointed under section 105 of that Act for that person, he shall be deemed to be a receiver appointed under section 99 of this Act for that person and shall continue to have the same functions in relation to that person's property and affairs as were exercisable by him

immediately before the commencement of that Act as committee of the estate and references in any document to the committee of the estate of that person shall be construed accordingly.

45 Section 101(1) of this Act shall apply in relation to any disposal of property (within the meaning of that section) of a person living on 1st November 1960, being a disposal effected under the Lunacy Act 1890 as it applies in relation to the disposal of property of a person effected under Part VII of this Act.

46 For the purposes of section 15 of the National Health Service Reorganisation Act 1973 (preservation of certain boards of governors) any provision of this Act which corresponds to a provision amended by that Act shall be treated as if it were such a provision and any reference in any order for the time being in force under that section to such a provision shall have effect as if it were a reference to the corresponding provision of this Act.

## SCHEDULE 6

Section 134.

### Repeals

| Chapter | Short title | Extent of repeal |
|---|---|---|
| 7 & 8 Eliz. 2. c. 72. | The Mental Health Act 1959. | Sections 1 to 5. |
| | | Section 10. |
| | | Section 22. |
| | | Sections 25 to 35. |
| | | Sections 37 to 43. |
| | | Sections 45 to 60. |
| | | Sections 62 to 68. |
| | | Sections 70 to 76. |
| | | Sections 80 and 81. |
| | | Section 85. |
| | | Section 87. |
| | | Sections 89 and 90. |
| | | Sections 92 to 96. |
| | | Sections 99 to 119. |
| | | Sections 121 to 126. |
| | | Sections 129 and 130. |
| | | Sections 132 and 133. |
| | | Sections 135 to 141. |
| | | In section 144, in subsection (1), paragraph (b). |

| Chapter | Short title | Extent of repeal |
|---|---|---|
| | | Section 145(2). |
| | | Sections 147 and 148. |
| | | Section 149(3) to (5). |
| | | In section 150, the words from " section ten " to " section one hundred and forty one " and from "section one hundred and forty six " to " Schedules ". |
| | | In section 152, the words from " sections eighty-five" to " Northern Ireland by that section ", from " section one hundred and twenty-nine " to " Schedules " and the words "Part II of the Seventh Schedule; Part 11 of the Eighth Schedule ". |
| | | Section 153. |
| | | Schedule 1. |
| | | Schedule 3. |
| | | Schedule 5. |
| | | Schedule 6, except paragraph 15(4). |
| | | In Schedule 7, in Part 1 the entry relating to sections 48 and 49 of the Fines and Recoveries Act 1833 and in Part 11 the entries relating to the Polish Resettlement Act 1947 and the USA Veterans' Pensions (Administration) Act 1949. |
| 1960 c. 61. | The Mental Health (Scotland) Act 1960. | Section 74. |
| | | In Schedule 4, all the entries relating to the Mental Health Act 1959 except those relating to section 9 and Schedule 7. |
| 1961 (N.I.) c. 15. | The Mental Health Act (Northern Ireland) 1961. | In Schedule 5, paragraphs 1 to 4. |
| 1964 c. 84. | The Criminal Procedure (Insanity) Act 1964. | Section 4(7). |

| Chapter | Short title | Extent of repeal |
|---|---|---|
| 1965 c. 2. | The Administration of Justice Act 1965. | In Schedule 1, the entry relating to the Mental Health Act 1959. |
| 1968 c. 20. | The Courts-Martial (Appeals) Act 1968. | In Schedule 4, the entry relating to the Mental Health Act 1959. |
| 1968 c. 49. | The Social Work (Scotland) Act 1968. | In Schedule 8, paragraphs 48 and 49. |
| 1969 c. 46. | The Family Law Reform Act 1969. | In Schedule 1 the entries relating to the Mental Health Act 1959. |
| 1969 c. 54. | The Children and Young Persons Act 1969. | In Schedule 5, paragraphs 38 to 40. |
| 1969 c. 58. | The Administration of Justice Act 1969. | Sections 17 to 19. |
| 1970 c. 42. | The Local Authority Social Services Act 1970. | In Schedule 1, the entry relating to the Mental Health (Amendment) Act 1982. |
| 1971 c. 23. | The Courts Act 1971. | In Schedule 8, paragraph 38. In Part I of Schedule 9, the entry relating to the Mental Health Act 1959. |
| 1971 c. 77. | The Immigration Act 1971. | In section 30(2), the words from " and accordingly" onwards. |
| 1972 c. 70. | The Local Government Act 1972. | In Schedule 23, in paragraph 9, in sub-paragraph (1) the words " 35, 56(2)(c) and 56(3) ", in sub-paragraph (2) the words " 10(1), 22, 27(2), 33, 34, 38(3), 40 to 43, 47(2), 52, 53, 59, 60" and "132", sub-paragraphs (4), (5) and (6). |
| 1973 c. 29. | The Guardianship Act 1973. | In section 1(8), the words from "and" to the end of the subsection. |
| 1975 c. 37. | The Nursing Homes Act 1975. | In Schedule 1, paragraphs 1 to 4. |
| 1977 c. 45. | The Criminal Law Act 1977. | In Schedule 6, the entry relating to section 130(3) of the Mental Health Act 1959. |

| Chapter | Short title | Extent of repeal |
|---|---|---|
| 1977 c. 49. | The National Health Service Act 1977. | In section 105(3), the words "or the Mental Health Act 1959". |
| | | In Schedule 15, paragraphs 23, 26 to 28, 30, 31 and 33. |
| 1978 c. 29. | The National Health Service (Scotland) Act 1978. | In paragraph 10(b) of Schedule 15, the figure" 102". |
| 1980 c. 5. | The Child Care Act 1980. | In Schedule 5, paragraphs 13 and 14. |
| 1980 c. 43. | The Magistrates' Courts Act 1980. | In Schedule 7, paragraphs 31 and 32. |
| 1980 c. 53. | The Health Services Act 1980. | In Schedule 1, paragraph 13. |
| 1981 c. 45. | The Forgery and Counterfeiting Act 1981. | Section 11(1). |
| 1981 c. 54. | The Supreme Court Act 1981. | Section 144. |
| | | In Schedule 5, paragraphs 2 and 3 of the entry relating to the Mental Health Act 1959. |
| | | In Schedule 6, paragraph 4. |
| 1981 c. 61. | The British Nationality Act 1981. | In section 39(7) the words " section 90 of the Mental Health Act 1959 and ". |
| 1982 c. 51. | The Mental Health (Amendment) Act 1982. | Sections 1 to 33. |
| | | Sections 35 to 61. |
| | | In section 63, subsection (1) and in subsection (2) the words from the beginning to " Act and ". |
| | | Section 64(1), (2), (3), (5) and (6). |
| | | Section 66. |
| | | Section 68(2) and (3). |
| | | Section 69(2), (3), and (4). |
| | | In section 70(2), the words " sections 35(1) and (2) and 64(6) above extend to Northern Ireland ". |
| | | Schedule 1. |

| Chapter | Short title | Extent of repeal |
|---|---|---|
| | | In Schedule 3, in Part I paragraphs 1 to 26, in paragraph 35 sub-paragraph (a), paragraphs 40, 42, 45 and 46, in paragraph 50 sub-paragraph (a), in paragraph 51 sub-paragraph (a), paragraphs 52 to 55, 57 and 58 and Part II.<br>In Schedule 5, paragraphs 2 to 15. |

Adapted and published by GRANGIS under the OGL Licence 3.0.

www.nationalarchives.gov.uk/doc/open-government-licence/version/3/

GRANGIS - UK PUBLISHING 2022.

Thank you for taking the time to leave us a review regarding this version

★★★★★

For further inquiries, contact us at:
www.grangis.com / contact@grangis.com

www.ingramcontent.com/pod-product-compliance
Lightning Source LLC
LaVergne TN
LVHW060213210926
848481LV00008B/2718
* 9 7 9 8 8 8 5 5 9 0 2 7 3 *